the little book of
self-care
for
new mums

Beccy Hands and
Alexis Stickland

Alexis Stickland is a midwife, antenatal teacher and mother of three children who has been supporting new mums for over 12 years.

Beccy Hands is a doula and remedial massage therapist specialising in pre- and post-natal wellbeing, who has been supporting women since 2003.

Together they founded *The Mother Box* in 2017, a company that supports new mums with essential advice and nurturing wellbeing gift boxes.

....

10

Vermilion, an imprint of Ebury Publishing,
20 Vauxhall Bridge Road,
London, SW1V 2SA

Vermilion is part of the Penguin Random House group of companies whose addresses can be found at global.penguinrandomhouse.com

 Penguin
Random House
UK

First published by Vermilion in 2018
www.penguin.co.uk

A CIP catalogue record for this book is available from the British Library

Commissioning Editor: Samantha Jackson
Project Editor: Laura Herring
Designer: Laura Liggins
Illustrator: Kay Barker

ISBN 9781785041822

Printed and bound in China by Toppan Leefung

Penguin Random House is committed to a sustainable future for our business, our readers and our planet. This book is made from Forest Stewardship Council® certified paper.

MIX
Paper from
responsible sources
FSC
www.fsc.org   FSC® C018179

Contents:

Megatron
from *Nobody Told Me* by Hollie McNish

He said
Megatron's the best one
if I was one, it's him.
Optimus Prime's all nice and stuff
but it's Megatron who really wins.

I've listened so many times to this
since last week's sodding
    Transformers hit
and I smile until today I say
Megatron ain't shit
last year my hip bones moved
another half an inch
back together.

He said
Hollie — Megatron lives for ever.
I said
Megatron's not real!
If you wanna see a real
    live transformer
come and have a feel!

And I pushed his fingers closer
and then right inside my stomach
to feel the gap my muscles left
from something I now know a bit as
birth

And I knew that this would hurt
but I did not know the rest
That there's a hole inside
        my stomach
till the day I'm laid to rest

And no, you're right I said
It's not the same
I did not turn into a car —
I turned into a factory
A life support and cooker

As my body started morphing
My insides realigned
My digestive system shifted
And completely redesigned itself
No help from the Decepticons or
        the Autobots

What vitamins I'd got
moved from my blood into hers now
The direction of my nutrients
redirected into her. How?
I don't know!

Everyone sees our stomachs grow
They do not see the rest
Ribcages cranking up
to make more space for baby's legs

Diaphragm moves down
Your womb fills up with fluid
and a brown line on your
                    skin appears
and no one even drew it!

A brown line on your skin!
From between your legs to boobs
The only line a child can see
to lead them to the food

Labour came and went
Something that I won't forget
Baby now in my arms
and my system shifted once again

Digestion redirected to
two breasts that grew one night
bigger than a large ripe pair
                    of cantaloupes

Get me a pump! I screamed
Genuinely worried that they
                    might explode

My boobs stay warm to heat
                    the milk
and my nipple makes a hole
and every time the baby drinks
the suction
makes my:

Womb shrink back
My hips move back
My ribs and diaphragm move back
My hair grow back
My back stretch back

And after two more years of
                    doing that
My system shifted back
Nutrients shot back into my own
                    body's blood again

And now I'm almost back to how
                    I was
before that seed took life
*Complete transformation without
                    one single robot fight
And no one makes an action film
                    of this!*

In fact all my body has to show for it
are the markings on my belly
My hips bones stayed a bit apart
and my breasts are slightly saggy

But the saddest thing of all
is that we're told these marks are *bad*
but they're the only few reminders
of this process we all have

as the real lifetime transformers
I'm saying *Megatron ain't shit*
Compared to female bodies
to prepare to grow and feed a kid

and the only thing our body's given
for this Optimus of Primes
Is a pot of sodding stretch-
                    mark cream
— to try to hide the signs.

welcome to
motherhood

From sore breasts to tender bottoms, extreme tiredness to anxious insomnia, we've seen it all. Over our combined years working as a midwife and doula, we have sat beside hundreds of women as they journeyed into the world of motherhood. We have celebrated with families as they welcomed their little ones into the world, watched our ladies transform into mothers and marvelled over the tiny humans they created. But we have also wiped away plenty of tears, given out hugs and offered heaps of TLC. We have made endless cups of tea, lactation biscuits, hot buttered toast and iron-boosting smoothies for tired new mums who sometimes just, you know, need a break.

Over more than a decade spent with amazing mums just like you – and from looking after our own typically unpredictable newborns – we have collected many a trick up our sleeves to help ease those postnatal discomforts and new-mum worries. We have tucked mums up in bed when they needed to rest, shown them gentle stretches to soothe their aching muscles, and nagged them when they haven't been eating properly.

While you were pregnant, you probably read at least one book on what to expect during those nine long months. And then there were the apps to track your trimesters, the regular midwife appointments, antenatal classes, scans, check-ups, pregnancy yoga classes and all your new fellow preggo friends

to talk to about how you are feeling – with maybe the odd cheeky massage or pedicure along the way to treat yourself when things got a bit much (well, you can't reach your toes, can you?!). While you were pregnant it was all about you and how best to look after yourself and stay healthy and relaxed to provide for your growing baby.

However, once your baby is born, it is really noticeable to us how the focus shifts dramatically to 'parenting' and the needs of your little one. There are hundreds of books available on how to raise your child and the developmental milestones your baby will go through during their first year, and you'll probably find that most of your local postnatal classes are very baby-focused too. It seems to us that somehow society has forgotten about the sensitive needs of our new mums. Where did their care go and why is there no longer any focus on them?

Just because your baby has now been born, he or she still relies on you 24/7. So it's just as important that you continue to care for yourself just as you did in pregnancy. By giving you the tools and knowledge to take care of your postnatal body and mind, we hope you will feel empowered to practise the self-care you need. Be kind to yourself as you adjust to this momentous experience. Our motivation is always to hold you tightly, to ensure you feel supported and nurtured, so you can really enjoy those early weeks and months of getting to know your new baby – just how it was always meant to be.

We know that those early, hazy days can be incredible and beautiful but they can also be overwhelming and exhausting. They can feel as if they are happening outside of time and space, where days and nights merge, our bodies don't feel like our own and our lives have been turned upside down. As time passes, you will adapt and you will begin to feel a little bit more in control – we promise! But be patient with yourself and your baby. Don't try and rush the process.

We've divided the book into three key chapters: Healing a Mother, Minding a Mother and Guiding a Mother. To us, these represent the essential areas of recovery and adjustment in the postnatal period.

In Healing a Mother, we share our tips for those days and weeks immediately following the birth, and then on throughout the months that follow. It won't surprise you that we are not coy about the subject of lady bits; we talk you through the changes that are happening in your body, including down below. Regardless of how you birthed your baby, your postnatal body is going to take time to heal and it is helpful to be responsive and sensitive to your needs during this time. We have also included some fantastic easy stretches, massage techniques and a simple restorative yoga sequence. Dip in and out of these when you need to combat any aches and pains from carrying that lovely little bundle!

As you and your brand-new baby spend precious time together during the initial settling-in months, it can be easy to forget to nourish yourself properly because your focus is on making sure your little one is getting all that they need. We have lost count of the number of new mums and dads we see existing on toast and the odd takeaway. However, it is very difficult to care for someone else when your own fuel tank is running on empty. Although the occasional packet of biscuits is a new mother's prerogative, filling yourself up the right way will really boost your energy levels and help you feel healthy and well – and you'll also be better able to cope if things get a little tough. We don't expect you to spend hours in the kitchen cooking up a feast when you have an adorable newborn to cuddle and you haven't had a full night's sleep for what seems like forever! Instead, we have plenty of totally delicious and nutritious yet completely effortless ideas for smoothies, snacks and hearty meals to help you regain that pre-baby spring in your step.

We also want to help you acknowledge the huge adaptations your mind makes when you become a mum, so we have a whole chapter devoted to this in Minding a Mother. For some mums, adapting to a life of caring for a baby around the clock comes very naturally, but for many of us, our minds need a little bit of time to catch up with this monumental gear shift. We now know that the mind and body are not separate from one another. They can both directly affect how the other copes with the changes that being a new parent brings. There are so many ways we can help ourselves adjust to our new 'Mum' identity, navigate the challenges to our relationships and regain control in those overwhelming moments. In this important chapter, we have included lots of practical tips to help calm the mind, including a guided relaxation and some simple breathing techniques.

Finally, in Guiding a Mother, we offer up the best of our practical experience in the form of how-to advice and ideas to address those hot topics all new mums face. We cover the difficulties of feeding, how to cope during the long, late nights while your partner sleeps on obliviously beside you, and how and when to rediscover your inner sex goddess (she still exists, don't worry!) and get back in the sack.

But, despite our experience, know that your way is best – you know more than you think you do, so trust your mother's intuition (we discuss this too). We offer up suggestions that we hope will help, but remember to treat them as just that; as the chapter title suggests, this is a guide, not a manual.

We will also harp on all the way through this book about the absolute need to take rest wherever you can – we know caring for a new baby can be exhausting! We have spent years working with frazzled new mums and have experienced that deep level of tiredness first-hand so we know what you're going through. We share our tips for navigating sleepless nights, and suggest how to reframe the way you rest, nap and sleep so you can get more much-needed kip.

The twelve-week period following the birth is now often talked about as the 'fourth trimester' – when mum, baby and the rest of the family take time to get to know their new family member, rest up and recover. We honestly believe that if new mums understood that it would take at least three months for their bodies to recover and readjust, they wouldn't be so hard on themselves and might take things more slowly – and even enjoy their postnatal body.

More than anything, though, we want this book to bring a smile to your face. We want you to know that you are brilliant and you're doing an incredible job. If you ever feel alone as you embark on your one-millionth night-time feed, staring out the window at the moon with just next-door's cat prowling the garden for company, know that there are women around the world doing exactly what you are doing right now. Giving yourself some self-care is not an indulgence, it is a necessity. You are responsible for the wellbeing of a tiny new person, so make sure you look after yourself properly so you can support them as best you can.

It is an absolute honour for us to play a small part in your postnatal journey. We hope this book helps you to feel cared for, celebrated and truly looked after. We want you to pick it up any time you could do with some extra support and encouragement when it comes to caring for and nuturing your postnatal mind and body. Our mission is for you to have the most enjoyable postnatal journey possible, to help you appreciate all those fleeting precious moments with your newborn. We want you to be aware of practical ways to care for yourself, to know when to reach out for support and to feel confident in yourself as you start out on this fun, exhilarating, sometimes challenging and endlessly rewarding journey of motherhood.

healing

a mother

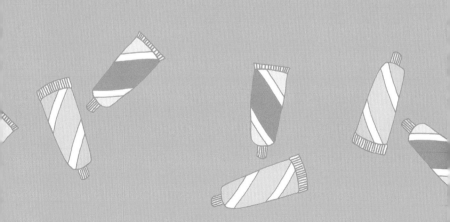

Whether you birthed vaginally or abdominally, you did it. Well done you! You should be incredibly proud of yourself. Now you are a mum, we know how busy life can get but here is our plea to you: take care of yourself first. You have just grown and birthed a baby and your body will be tired, wired and incredibly overwhelmed so you need time to rest, to heal and to get to know your new family member. Your postnatal recovery should be prioritised above any household chore or social event.

The female body is incredible. When you really consider it, the fact that you had the ability to grow an actual human being from scratch is mind-blowing. Even more fascinating still is the fact that apart from taking your vitamins, being careful about what you ate and perhaps giving your mind time to be calm and relaxed, your body did the lion's share of the work, ALL BY ITSELF.

Now you find yourself on the other side of your birthing story. You are a mother with a babe in arms, sensitive breasts and a gigantic maternity pad in place. Following the birth of your baby you may be surprised just how open and tender you feel both mentally and physically as you adjust to motherhood and your body heals from pregnancy and birth. You may find you are very sensitive to light, noise and touch as your body is hypervigilant, preparing you to care for your baby's every need, and as your hormones settle, so too will these feelings.

In recent decades, we seem to have acquired a stoic response to the transition to motherhood. It seems that 'bouncing back' as quickly as possible is the goal and many women feel pressure to just 'get on with it' without making a fuss. However, it really isn't helpful to put such pressure on a brand-new mother who is in the midst of the biggest change, both physically and mentally, that a woman can go through.

The postnatal period is generally considered to be the six weeks immediately following giving birth. In reality, we consider a mum to be postnatal for up to eighteen months afterwards, as this is the length of time it can often take mothers to really feel like they have regained their energy and physical normality. How a woman heals and restores from birth is as individual as we all are. There is no 'one size fits all' to your postnatal healing process. Take the time you need.

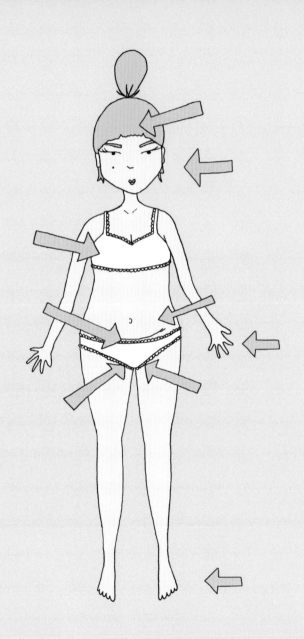

Understanding Your Postnatal Body

So, which parts of our body require an extra dose of TLC post birth and how can we support them as we morph into a new postnatal version of ourselves? Understanding what happens to our bodies after birth and knowing how to soothe ourselves makes for a much more enjoyable postnatal period.

Uterus/womb

At full capacity, the uterus is the largest muscle in either the female or male body. Immediately after giving birth, the uterus contracts significantly, encouraging the release and birth of the placenta. Once the uterus is effectively 'emptied', the uterine fibres contract further and over the course of the next seven to ten days it returns to the clenched fist-sized muscle of its non-pregnant state. During your postnatal visits, your midwife will ask if she can touch your tummy and feel where the uterus is to check that it is indeed returning back to where it was pre-pregnancy. The fab thing about the uterus is that is heals itself brilliantly after birth; however, you can aid this healing process by drinking raspberry leaf tea, for example, which is a great uterine tonic (see our tea section on pages 74–75 for more info).

Vagina

Post birth you will have vaginal blood loss. This is a normal process that occurs no matter how you birthed your baby as it comes from the uterus lining where your placenta has been released, which is now starting to heal and renew. At first, directly after the placenta is born, there is likely to be heavy blood loss. (But if you are concerned, do ask for your midwife's advice.) As the weeks continue, you will notice the loss lessens and the colour starts to change from dark red to pale pink before stopping completely. This can last up to four to six weeks. During this time, you will need to wear a maternity pad and some nice big pants to keep it in place. As the blood lessens you can switch to a normal maternity towel, but we recommend keeping the big pants! Not only are they good for holding pads in place, but they will feel supportive and less tight on sensitive tummies and tender bits.

C-section scar

Caesarean sections now account for approximately a quarter of all births in the UK. The recovery period (up to six weeks) needs to be honoured as your body has been through significant abdominal surgery. We appreciate that this is easier said than done when you also have a newborn to care for but just consider for a moment how you would nurture and care for your body if you had been through ANY other form of operation. It is so important to be gentle with yourself and accept as much support as possible in those early days and weeks. As your muscles knit back together and your wound heals, be very careful about the weight of items that you carry. As a guide, we suggest you hold nothing heavier than your baby. Remember, even if you have not birthed vaginally, you still need to be mindful of your pelvic floor and perineum, as you will not initially have the core strength to support them fully (see opposite). We have had many clients who were shocked by vaginal soreness even though they didn't have a vaginal birth; this is caused by low postnatal levels of oestrogen, which effects the elasticity of the vaginal tissues. Also see page 44 for more on C-section aftercare.

Pelvic floor

When you think about your pelvic floor, it is useful to think of it as a bunch of muscles, all working together to create a muscular hammock running from the front of your pelvis across to your tail bone. However you birthed your baby, your pelvic floor will need some TLC in the postnatal period to help it regain its tone and strengthen it following the added strain caused by the weight of your growing baby during pregnancy. We know us midwives bang on about pelvic floor exercises in the postnatal period, but it really is important to care for these muscles at this point if you don't want to pee every time you sneeze. (See pages 26–27 for more pelvic floor self-care advice.)

Perineum

The perineum is the area between the vagina and the anus. It is fairly common to experience a tear or grazing in this area during birth, especially if it is your first vaginal delivery. You may even have had a little cut to your perineum to help make some extra room to birth your baby. If so, you will have had stitches and you will be advised to take pain relief to keep you as comfortable as possible. Whether you needed stitches or not, though, you are likely to feel tender, swollen and bruised initially after birth. If you have experienced a more advanced tear you may also be taking a course of antibiotics to help avoid an infection occurring, and laxatives to prevent you becoming constipated. Try using a peri bottle when you go to the toilet, make some of our soothing pads or take a sitz bath to ease discomfort (see pages 34–35).

Boobs

Most women will notice changes happening in their breasts during pregnancy. The breast tissue may become fuller and the areola and nipple may appear darker in colour. (It is thought that this very clever adaptation occurs in order to make your areola easier for your baby to see and aim for as a target!) It is also possible that you have been expressing small amounts of milk during the last few weeks of pregnancy. In the first few days following birth, with a baby that is encouraged to breastfeed and with the added postnatal surge of the hormones oxytocin and prolactin, your breasts will produce colostrum. Around days 3–5, you will start to notice your breasts feeling fuller and heavier as the colostrum changes into the more mature milk, which is lighter in colour and has a more watery consistency. As the milk comes in, our breasts can become tender as they get used to how much milk they need to make. Our hormones also rise, causing us to feel weepy – but, once again, this will settle. We have lots of tips on soothing tender breasts (see pages 40–43 and pages 55 and 162–165 for more info on breastfeeding).

Fluid retention

Oedema is the medical term for swelling, and postnatal oedema is very common. It is caused by a combination of hormonal changes, extra blood and natural and intravenous fluid retention. Most women who have a C-section receive medication and anaesthesia through an IV and those who give birth vaginally may receive medication and other fluids this way too. These extra fluids tend to accumulate in the body, typically in the hands, face, legs, feet and pelvis and can take several days to leave your body. However, if you notice excess swelling, please consult your midwife as soon as possible. You will feel the need to wee frequently as your body removes the excess fluids. Paradoxically, you actually need to drink more fluids to help your body get rid of excess fluids. See page 36 for more tips to get you peeing!

Haemorrhoids

Haemorrhoids – or piles as they are often called – are swollen veins found around the anus and lower rectum. They are common in pregnancy and the postnatal period. Most women will experience them at some point, yet nobody talks about them! Why are we all so bottom shy?! If you are experiencing a sore and itchy bottom, little hanging lumps around the anus or bleeding when you have a bowel movement, then it is likely that you are suffering with these unpleasant little beasts. Keep hydrated and up your fibre intake to help you stay regular. If you are experiencing any discomfort from haemorrhoids, see our ways to soothe irritation on pages 38–39. If you are feeling bloated and uncomfortable from constipation and nothing else is working, visit your GP and get prescribed a laxative and poo softener.

Hormones

Our hormones are incredible: they create the perfect environment for conception, support our baby as he or she grows, and our bodies as we change shape. They are the key ingredient for triggering labour and they then turn our bodies into milk machines. However, they can also leave us very emotionally wobbly. High as a kite one minute, feeling completely loved-up and euphoric, then tumbling down with a crash into a tearful heap. Add to that the joy of night sweats and leaking breasts and you may find you don't quite know what to do with yourself. FEAR NOT! Your hormones will resettle. You can also try natural remedies and therapies such as acupuncture, homeopathy and reflexology to support this rebalancing process. And see our section on soothing teas on pages 74–75.

Hello, Down Below!

Let's just get to it, ladies. However you birthed your babies, we know what you're all thinking about.

When we are talking about 'down below' we are namely referring to the vagina, clitoris, labia, perineum and anus. All the sensitive parts of you that have been stretched, squeezed and pulled during pregnancy and birth. You may find that you're very aware of how different you feel in and around your vagina as it is healing. The swelling and bruising in particular can feel quite odd and uncomfortable at times. Many women who have had Caesarean sections are surprised at how tender they can feel too – and hormonal dryness, swelling and pelvic floor issues are common across the board.

Following the birth, you may avoid thinking about what is going on down there. It may seem too soon to take a look at your bits, especially in those initial postnatal days. However, it often feels worse than it looks and when you are ready it can be reassuring to pop a little mirror down there after a shower. It is really useful and important to be aware of what is going on, as it can help you notice when things don't look or feel quite right. Then you can tell your midwife and she can take a look and assess how the healing is going.

You are likely to feel swollen and bruised the first week or so after the birth in this whole area. You may have a tear that has affected your vagina, clitoris, labia, perineum and/or anus. Or you may have had a small cut in the perineum to make the birth a little easier (episiotomy). If you experienced either of these, then you may have a few sutures (stitches) too. This is all likely to make you feel extremely sensitive initially and you may have been given a cocktail of pain relief and perhaps some laxative medications to help you to be as comfortable as possible.

As your muscles and/or skin start to knit back together and the sutures dissolve in the following weeks, it can start to feel tight and itchy. This is a perfectly normal part of the healing process – the body cleverly seals itself in order to protect you from infection. If the itching is accompanied by an unpleasant-smelling discharge, though, this could be a sign of an infection and you should visit your GP.

Follow this advice to keep your lady garden blooming happily:

- Keep this area clean and dry to aid the healing process. Shower daily, as you would normally, being careful to clean below without being too heavy-handed. After washing, pat the area dry with a clean towel and make sure you pop a clean maternity pad into your comfortable big pants.

- As mentioned above, pants should be big, comfy and high-waisted so there is no pressure on your lower abdomen, especially if you have had a C-section. Stick to natural fibres to allow your bits to breathe and avoid possible irritation as your skin will be more sensitive after birth.

- Concentrated urine can sting and burn as it passes over your stitches, so use a peri bottle in those early days (see page 34). Then pat dry and change your maternity pad as above.

- If you are worried that something does not feel right, is painful or smells offensive, always mention it to your midwife or GP. It may be that you have a little infection in your stitches and you need some antibiotics to help with the healing.

- Haemorrhoids (piles) can make an appearance in pregnancy and can be exacerbated during birth, leaving you feeling itchy, sore and very uncomfortable. These pesky swollen veins around the anus or lower rectum can be inside or outside the anus and hang there like a small bunch of tiny grapes. The good news is that you absolutely can treat these little blighters and there are many ways to soothe the discomfort (see pages 38–39).

- If you are concerned by a bulging sensation from the vagina or feel a bit like you are wearing a tampon when you are not – or perhaps you notice something protruding from your vagina, you could be experiencing a prolapse. This occurs when the pelvic floor becomes weakened and is not supporting the internal organs as it should. If you are uncomfortable, leaking urine or just curious whether this has happened to you, please do not hesitate to get checked out by your GP. If you have had a prolapse, you are likely to be encouraged to carry on with your pelvic floor exercises (see pages 26–27) as these can make a huge difference. You may also need to see a women's health physiotherapist to help build up your core strength, which helps the pelvic floor support everything above it.

Pelvic Floor Exercises

However you are feeling down below, doing your pelvic floor exercises every day can really help you regain that all-important core strength. The pelvic floor is part of the core muscles and it is these muscles that will help lift your pelvic organs back into position. Below, Emma Fulwood – MUTU Pro (personal trainer to postnatal mums) talks us through her fantastic breathing sequence to help get the pelvic floor working as a whole system of core muscles, reconnecting these muscles and supporting the body as it recovers from the stress of pregnancy and childbirth. Remember, though, these exercises are not only for the postnatal period, but are good practise for life and ongoing pelvic health.

- First make sure you are in good alignment, so whether you are sitting, standing or lying down, try and stack your ribs in line with your hip bones. If your ribs are thrusting forward, then the pelvic floor can't work as it should. The same happens if you are slouching. Good alignment enables the whole core system to co-ordinate and work together as it should.

- Without altering your alignment, let go of any grip in your abdominals and pelvic floor. Often, we hold in our abdominals to make them appear flatter, and we also hold up our pelvic floor when tense or we fear we may leak. Learning to let go of the grip in both abdominals and pelvic floor is vital to obtaining a co-ordinated pelvic floor and a stronger core system.

- Inhale through your nose. Notice when you inhale whether your shoulders are raising up. Try to stop this from happening by focusing on the ribcage expanding out to the side and the back. As you inhale also focus on letting go of the grip in your abdominals and your pelvic floor lowering; you can't breathe properly if you aren't releasing the grip.

- As you exhale, focus on bringing the pelvic floor muscles together and closing and lifting them.

- Repeat: inhale and relax the pelvic floor muscles, then exhale and bring them together and gently lift them.

Try and focus on this type of breath pattern twice a day for around five minutes, breathing in and out steadily. You might find that, at first, you want to do things backwards and inhale while you pull up the pelvic floor. Don't panic! Just keep practising and it will soon start to feel familiar.

If you are more of a visual person – you might prefer to try approaching the exercise this way:

- Visualise your pelvic floor as a lift. Take a big breath in and imagine people getting in on the ground floor! As you breathe out slowly, pull up to the first floor. When pulling up, squeeze the muscles as if your are trying to stop passing wind and urine flow. Hold for three, then pull up to the second floor as you continue to breathe out. Hold for three, and pull up to the third floor while breathing out. Hold it there while the people get out! Then fully breathe out.

- On the in breath, do the reverse (lowering the lift in stages).

- Start with four repetitions three times a day, and gradually increase as your strength builds.

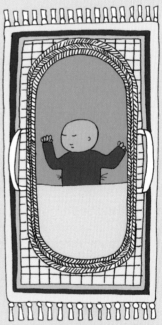

The Importance of Rest, Part 1

In many non-Western cultures around the world a new mother is encouraged to spend her first postnatal weeks – up to sixty days in some countries! – devoted entirely to resting, feeding herself and her baby and bonding with her new bundle of joy. She is relieved of all household chores, fed restorative meals by her community and refrains from having sex. Mum is encouraged to take as much time as she needs to heal properly, so she can restore her energy and focus on caring for her baby. In Japan, it is still customary for a new mum to move back in with her parents and spend twenty-one days in bed. While this may not appeal to our Western lifestyles, we can certainly learn from this! Not only does this special time allow for mum and baby to recover, it also helps mum feel supported and nurtured by those around her.

We know that Western culture isn't set up for women to have long periods of confinement after birth, but it is so important that you try to take the time to rest up properly and find ways to give yourself the self-care you need. We understand that without living in large communities, as other cultures do, or with extended family nearby it is very difficult to take time to rest and heal. But we can also see that our current set-up, with many mums parenting in isolation, isn't working. We have a high number of mums suffering with postnatal depression and anxiety compared to cultures where mothers are nurtured and held, with care and company, in their early mothering journey.

Top tips for going to sleep quickly, day or night:

In those early weeks, the days and nights often merge into one. We have to try to grasp that all-important rest whenever possible to help us function. Sleeping when baby sleeps is one of the best ways to stop ourselves spiralling into complete exhaustion, but it is easier said than done.

There is often a list of chores we want to complete while the little one naps or it may be that we are so wired and overtired that we cannot switch our minds off to take advantage of a little daytime shut-eye. Worry not, we have put together some ways to help calm the mind and relax your healing postnatal body ready for some restorative sleep, day or night. Also see pages 154–158 for more on sleep . . . Zzzzz.

1. **Get comfy:** Even though you may not know how long you will manage to sleep for, get your cosiest PJs on, snuggle down in bed and get totally comfortable, even if it is daytime. It is hard to rest while your tight jeans or overly snug bra are digging in and making you feel ill at ease.

2. **Lavender spritz:** Lavender is well known for its relaxing effect on the body and mind. Buy a pillow spritz online, or make your own cheap and easy version: buy an empty spritz bottle and fill it with water, add ten drops of lavender essential oil, give it a shake and spray the calming mist around. After 24–48 hours, make a fresh batch as it will lose its potency.

3. **Drink tea:** If you know your baby tends to fall asleep while feeding, or straight after, make yourself a cup of tea that you can drink while they feed so that afterwards you're both ready for a kip. Teas that aid rest include chamomile, passionflower and lavender (see also pages 74–75).

4. **Scribble a chore list:** There will always be chores to be done. We totally understand how out of control your mind can feel when the house is a mess and the washing and laundry are mounting. It can feel never-ending. However, if you are totally depleted of energy, you need to be resting not rushing around tiring yourself out even more. Write down the things that are particularly important as this will help you feel more in control, then work through them when you are able to or split them up with your partner so they don't overwhelm you.

5. **Turn down the lights:** This sounds so obvious but sometimes we forget that in order to let our bodies rest and restore, we need to create the right environment, one where we feel safe, calm and relaxed. The absence of light sends an important message to our brain that it is time to sleep. This is also important for your baby. Try not to turn lights up too much at night as it can be very stimulating and make it more difficult for you to settle them after a feed or nappy change. It can also lead to your mind becoming overly alert and active.

5-MINUTE FIXES FOR FRAZZLED MUMS!

1. GET JIGGY WITH IT
Pop your baby in a sling, or hold them safely in your arms, play some uplifting music and move your gorgeous mama body to the beat. Dancing releases endorphins, which are immediate mood boosters. The movement will be calming and settling for your baby too. Win win!

2. DECLUTTER
Have a quick clear-up. It can have an immediate calming effect on the brain. This is not about cleaning the whole house, this is about just sorting out what is right in front of you right now.

3. PICK-YOU-UP PONGS
Essential oils are great mood boosters. You don't have to have any fancy kit, you can diffuse oil into your house using a good old-fashioned saucepan! Pop some water in the pan, bring to the boil, then turn the heat down and let it simmer. Add a few drops of your favourite oils and let the aroma lift your spirits. Great oils for mood boosting are sweet orange, lavender, lemon, geranium, neroli and rose. NB: Do not let it boil dry — top up the water if necessary.

4. 5-MINUTE MAKEOVER
If you haven't showered or washed your hair and your eye bags are down by your knees, treat yourself to this mini makeover:

- Flannel wash — cleanse pits, bits and breasts at the sink.
- Spritz your hair with dry shampoo and whack it up in a mum bun.
- Use some concealer and a bit of bronzer to lift your complexion.
- Finish with a splash of your favourite lippy.

5. MOOD-BOOSTING SMOOTHIES
See our favourite recipes on pages 66-67, but feel free to supplement any of the ingredients with something else delicious from your fridge.

6. MINDFULNESS
Pop on your headphones and listen to a quick mindfulness track. There

are loads online that will talk you through breathing, visualisation or scanning the body to release tension. Some of our favourites are:

- Headspace
- Simple Habit
- Quility
- Smiling Mind
- Calm

7. GET PLANNING

It's easy to get caught up in the daily grind of sleep times, nappy changes and feeding schedules. Get your diary out and plan some fun stuff that offers you a break from the routine. This can be just for you, or with your partner and baby. And it can be as little as a couple of hours or as big as a holiday. Having something fun to look forward to can help break up the monotony.

8. HAVE A BATH WITH BABY

Okay, so this might take a bit longer than 5 minutes but even a quick dip can make all the difference — soothing muscles and calming the mind. Having your baby in with you is not only a great way to get some endorphin-boosting skin-to-skin, it can also calm and settle a fractious baby. Follow your baby's lead and see how long they enjoy being in the bath

with you. Make sure you keep your baby cosy in lovely warm water (about 37°C, which is around body temperature).

9. STRETCHING

Feeding and carrying your new baby, coupled with night-time feeding and broken sleep, can cause havoc on the back and neck muscles. Tension in these areas can cause brain fog and low mood. Stretching is a wonderful way to move your body, breathe properly and release any tight muscles (see our easy stretches on pages 46-52).

10. WRITE A LIST

Sometimes when we try to do everything we can end up doing nothing! It all feels too much and can completely overwhelm us. Getting your to-do list down on paper immediately frees the mind up and can encourage a sense of calm and order. Look at the list and separate it into:

- Quick wins — easy jobs that leave you feeling lighter when achieved.
- Shared tasks — household chores and jobs that you can delegate or do together as a couple.
- Non-urgent — things that you want or need to do, but that aren't immediately necessary.

Easing Sore Parts

Episiotomy, vaginal tears, grazes and general stretching of the perineum all cause inflammation and sensitivity in the vaginal tissues. Try the following ways to ease discomfort:

Peri bottle

Use an old water bottle or plastic jug and fill it with warm water or lukewarm chamomile tea. Leave this beside the toilet and every time you pass urine, lean back as you wee and pour the water onto your vagina and perineum at the same time. This dilutes the acidity of the urine which stops any stinging and keeps the area clean. Gently pat dry (rather than wipe) with soft clean kitchen roll or a soft clean face cloth. Trust us, this is a very soothing pee-time ritual. You can add a little extra warm water if the solution has cooled and you don't fancy cold water on your sensitive parts!

Sitz bath

This is basically a shallow bath, with the water no higher than thigh height. It is a great way to cleanse underneath, especially if you've had a caesarean section and can't yet take a full bath.

1. Run a shallow bath (no higher than thigh height) and add 1 cup of Epsom salts, a jug of chamomile tea and 2 drops of lavender essential oil.

2. Sit in the shallow bath for 10 minutes and then carefully get out (if you have had a C-section you will need somebody to help you in and out of the bath) and gently pat yourself dry with a clean towel.

Cooling pads

Inflammation in your vulva
and perineal tissues can
cause heat, stinging and
soreness – not what you need
when you are trying to look
after a little one. Luckily, this
discomfort can be soothed
using a cold compress.

There are many types of
perineal cold packs for sale
out there, but you can make
your own inexpensive version
with some maternity pads
and a jug of chamomile tea!

1. Place 3 or 4 tea bags
    in a big jug, cover with
    boiling water and leave
    to steep for 30 minutes.

2. Place some of your
    maternity pads (the big
    bulky ones) on a kitchen
    tray or baking tray,
    making sure the part of
    the pad that touches the
    perineum is facing up.

3. Pour the tea over the
    pads, ensuring each
    one is fully soaked, then
    place the tray of pads
    into the fridge to cool
    for at least an hour.

4. To use a pad, place a
    thick folded towel or
    a waterproof sheet on
    your bed, chair or sofa.
    Place a pad inside your
    pants and sit on it. Enjoy
    the cooling relief while
    watching TV, feeding
    baby or reading a book.
    We always love the look
    of relief on a mum's face
    when she uses these
    pads, they really do
    feel great. After 10–20
    minutes, remove the pad
    and throw it away. Pat
    dry with a towel and pop
    on a fresh pair of pants.
    Repeat as needed.

Reducing Swelling and Water Retention

Extra blood, fluids and changing hormones can cause the extremities to swell after birth. This is called postnatal oedema and it should ease on its own within a week of giving birth. There are also some effortless ways to help encourage the body to let go of this excess fluid and ease the discomfort.

You need to pee

Drinking plenty of fluids and eating foods that act as a natural diuretic will really help your body to cleanse itself and get rid of excess fluid. Lots of women reduce their fluid intake thinking that this will help, but paradoxically you have to encourage your body to get rid of water by drinking more water. A new mum should be drinking at least eight to ten glasses a day, but the best way to gauge if you are getting enough is to check your pee. If it's clear, you are doing a good job of staying hydrated; if it's dark yellow, you need to drink more!

Natural diuretic foods

You could also try some natural diuretic foods to help encourage urination. These include apples, asparagus, beetroot, blueberries, celery, cherries, cucumber, grapes, green beans, lemons, parsley, pineapple, pumpkin, spinach and watercress. Also see our smoothie section on page 67 for a simple recipe to get the fluid flowing.

Herbal teas

Detoxifying herbal teas such as dandelion and nettle are also helpful in expelling excess fluid (see pages 74–75 for more on the power of herbal teas).

Check your posture

Avoid sitting with your legs or arms crossed for long periods of time, and make sure you get up and move around every time you go to the loo or at least once an hour to get the blood flowing.

Cabbage leaves

This may sound a bit mad but cabbage leaves are great at drawing out excess water. Pop a cabbage in the fridge to chill. Sit with your legs elevated and then wrap cabbage leaves over your legs and let the coolness soothe the swelling. The leaves will become wet as they draw out excess fluid (and through condensation); once this happens, discard and replace with some more chilled leaves.

Massage

Ask your partner to massage gently from your feet up towards your hips, using their hands only and in light stroking movements with gentle pressure. You are trying to stimulate the lymph system, which sits on top of the muscle and so a lighter pressure is best. (For more massage tips – including some self-massage ideas, see pages 56–59).

PLEASE NOTE:
Do not massage over inflamed varicose veins or any areas on the leg that are red and hot as this may be a sign of infection or a blood clot. Seek medical advice if any of these are present.

Sore Bottoms

Haemorrhoids (see page 21) are a pain in the bum – pun intended! Luckily, although piles are annoying, they are mostly quite easy to treat.

Cold pads
Use the cooling pads on page 35 to cool and soothe your bottom. You can add witch hazel astringent when making them to soothe any itching, or a couple of drops of tea tree essential oil for its antibacterial properties. If using essential oils, add to the chamomile tea mixture, then pour on to the pads to ensure it is diluted properly.

Stay regular
It's important to stay regular and not become constipated, as any straining will cause more inflammation and increase discomfort. Make sure you are eating lots of fibre-rich foods (fruit, veg and wholegrains) and drinking plenty of water. Constipation can also be caused by anxiety and lots of new mums are afraid of that First Postnatal Poo! However, postnatal constipation is very uncomfortable, so don't hold it in. The truth is, it's never as bad as you think it will be!

Here are some tips to help:

1. Don't rush. Allow yourself time and space to use the bathroom uninterrupted. If you can, hand baby over to your partner and take yourself away for some 'quiet time'. If you are on your own, let them have a lie down on a rug in the bathroom. If you try to rush you'll strain and if you strain it'll be sore.

2. Relax! And keep your mouth and jaw relaxed too. There is a neurological link between the mouth and

the sphincter muscles in the anus – so wiggle that jaw and relax your lips!

3. Supporting the perineum can help you to mentally relax the bowel. Use a clean wash cloth or maternity pad and hold it against the muscle between the vagina and bottom. You will likely feel your bowel relax immediately as your mind registers the support and the message that all is well to let go!

4. Also try placing your feet flat on a foot stool while you are on the loo so that your knees are higher than your hips. This position mimics squatting, which creates a better position to allow the bowels to open.

5. After each bowl movement, use a cooling pad or have a sitz bath to soothe and cleanse the area (see pages 35 and 34).

Push them back in

If your haemorrhoids are protruding from your bottom, the sensitive tissue that is used to being inside the body will become irritated and sore. The best thing you can do is to pop them back in after every bowel movement. We know this may not be your favourite way to spend an evening, but it'll ease discomfort dramatically, speed up healing time and reduce inflammation. Cleanse with a sitz bath and, with freshly washed fingers and a little oil such as coconut, grapeseed or even olive oil, gently push the pile(s) back up into your bottom.

PLEASE NOTE:
If your haemorrhoids continue to irritate you and cause you pain, please do see your GP.

Breasts

As your milk comes in around day 3–5, you will probably find yourself with full (read huge) and uncomfortable breasts. This, coupled with the milk hormones that make you feel like crying ALL of the time, can make for a pretty tough ride. But fear not – once again, some wonderful soothing pads can bring you lots of comfort! You can use them hot or cold.

Hot

To ease engorgement and encourage the milk to flow before a feed, use a hot wash cloth, or breast pad soaked in hot (NOT boiling) water and place it over the breast; if you want to hand express a little milk to ease the pressure you can do that now. You can also do this in a warm bath and use the shower head spray to warm and massage the breast (unless you are recovering from a Caesarean, see page 44).

Cold

Try using a cold breast pad after each feed to soothe hot sore breasts and reduce any inflammation and the sting that you might be feeling in your nipples as they adjust to breastfeeding. These pads are very similar to the cooling perineal pads (see page 35), but made with breast pads, and are an absolute lifesaver. Time and time again, our ladies say they honestly don't know what they would have done without them.

How to make and use cooling breast pads

Make these in the same way as the cooling perineal pads, ensuring that the waterproof backing is on the underside before you pour over the tea. Leave to cool on the tray for a couple of hours.

After a feed when your nipples are feeling sore or when your breasts are sore from engorgement, take a pad out of the fridge and place it inside your bra, so that it sits against the breast and cools it down. This is SO soothing and will take away any inflammation of the nipple. Throw the pad away after use, express a little milk, rub it around the nipple (milk is full of healing properties for the skin) and allow the breast to air-dry before putting your comfy bra on.

Breast combing

Mastitis is a condition that some women experience whereby the breast tissue of one breast becomes red, hard, inflamed and painful.

Mastitis can make you ache from top to toe as if you have the flu, experience hot flushes and cold chills and feel terribly unwell.

If you think this may be affecting you, contact your GP for support. They are likely to want to see you as soon as possible and if mastitis is confirmed they will offer you antibiotics. To help prevent mastitis, comb your breasts! Yep, we did say comb! This is a fabulous tip we learnt from a Japanese midwife many moons ago.

If your breasts are feeling engorged and lumpy or you have a hot red patch or lump then the chances are you will have areas of blocked, curdled milk. This is a perfect breeding ground for bacteria, which can then cause mastitis. Getting these

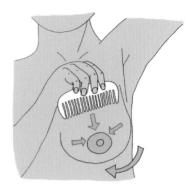

blockages moving will help stop mastitis in its tracks and often prevent it altogether.

At the first sign of a lump or red patch, before each feed, use an old gentleman's-style comb to comb the breast from the top down towards the nipple, all the way around the breast. Use a steady firm pressure, hard enough to feel that you are moving the flow, but not hard enough to hurt; the pressure should feel nice and soothing. Use a little oil to help the comb glide.

Latch baby for a feed; they will encourage milk to move through the breast and will suck out the curdled milk (it's totally safe, the bacteria

Chapped and cracked nipples

We have seen some incredibly sore nipples in our time working with new mums. There are few things less appealing for mum than latching a baby on to a sore, chapped and blistered nipple. The bottom line is if your breast is experiencing trauma to the tissue like this it is very likely the attachment of baby's mouth to your breast is not right. Seek out a good local breastfeeding clinic or lactation consultant or ask your health visitor for a list of local 'drop in' breastfeeding cafés, where a professional will be on hand to help you. Online videos can also help.

You can also use natural nipple creams but just be aware that if the attachment continues to be incorrect, then lotions will only help ease the complaint, rather than prevent it from reoccurring.

causing mastitis doesn't affect them at all). As baby feeds, continue to comb from armpit to nipple, focusing on the lumpy areas. You should start feeling relief quite quickly. Repeat this with every feed until the breast is soft and lump-free and any red patches have gone. Drink lots of warm water and herbal tea such as chamomile and nettle alongside combing, to flush general toxins from your system and keep yourself properly hydrated (see page 63 and our tea section on pages 74–75).

Caring for Yourself After a Caesarean Section

Follow the advice from your caregiver and take good care of your wound. Don't rush it! Here are our tips to help you heal.

- Keep the wound clean and dry and wear cotton high-waisted underwear. Shower only at first – check with your caregiver when you will be able to have bath.

- In the early days, limit anything that puts pressure on the abdominal wall, such as laughing, coughing or sneezing.

- If you are going to be a passenger in a car, take a pillow to use to protect your tummy from the seatbelt.

- You are more likely to experience constipation and wind after a C-section. Try using a hot water bottle (but not directly on the wound), as this can help ease discomfort, as can gentle circular massage in a clockwise direction, but again not directly on the wound. See also our smoothies and tea sections on pages 66–67 and 74–75.

- Once the wound has healed, gently massage your scar three times a day with a non-perfumed oil such as coconut or grapeseed oil to hydrate the skin and keep it supple. Use your fingertip in a circular motion, slowly but with firm pressure for 10–15 minutes.

- The scar is healed when the skin has sealed, the stitches have dissolved and any swelling and redness has disappeared. The scar site may still be tender for months after healing, so massage carefully and if it hurts, stop.

Get Your Sweat On

As your hormones settle and your body rids itself of excess fluid, you may experience lots more sweating. While annoying, it's completely normal and will pass. Leave a spare top by your bed to change into during the night if you wake up – cold sweat is not conducive to a good night's sleep! If you are hot, use a mister spray or a fan to keep you cool (make sure the fan isn't directly facing baby). If you are having cold sweats, a warm flannel on the forehead or back of the neck is very soothing.

General Muscle Aches

It is very common to feel achy after birth because your muscles have contracted and released lots of times to push your baby down into the birth canal. A lovely hot Epsom salts bath is a great way to ease tired aching muscles, reduce inflammation and fluid retention, promote healing of the perineum, alleviate tension headaches and soothe abdominal cramps. Follow the sitz bath instructions (see page 34), but fill the bath up as normal. For the lovely mamas who have had a C-section, unfortunately you will have to wait until the wound is completely healed until you can have a soak, which can take up to six weeks. During that time, take showers and make sure that your wound site is gently patted dry.

PLEASE NOTE:
Please avoid using Epsom salts if you had stitches after birth. Salt water may encourage dissolvable sutures to dissolve too quickly.

~ stretch it out ~

Being careful of your posture in the early postnatal weeks will help keep aches and pains to a minimum, but be mindful that it takes months for your core to strengthen again properly after birth. Remembering to engage these muscles before lifting baby or bending over the cot will help enormously.

We know that it's impossible to have perfect posture all the time and often we can be so desperate to get baby to feed so that they stop crying that we don't check we have enough pillows; or perhaps we are stooping forward, but we can't bear to move for fear that they'll stop feeding! We've all done it! But don't worry, we're here to help.

After you've had your first three weeks resting and sleeping as much as you can, from the fourth week, stretching is the key! Even if you've had the worst posture all day, eaten a whole packet of biscuits and your shoulders are up round you ears, all is not lost. Five minutes of stretching will encourage blood to flow through the body, relaxing and loosening tight muscles while giving you a little hit of oxytocin, which will help you feel calmer and more relaxed too.

Over the next few pages you'll find our favourite stretches to combat 'mum back', tight neck, hip ache, fatigue and brain fog. Try one or two a day to keep on top of tense muscles. Tack them on to something you already do, like brushing your teeth or waiting for the kettle to boil — maybe write 'STRETCH' on a sticky note and place it by your toothbrush or the kettle. This will be a reminder to stretch morning and night — or several times a day if you drink as much tea as us!

side neck stretch ~

This is a lovely stretch to relax the head, neck and jaw and for releasing tension caused by feeding and carrying baby. It is good for headaches too!

1. Lean sideways against a wall, letting your body weight trap your shoulder against the wall.

2. Reach your outside arm over and hold on to the far side of your head. Take a big breath in, and then on the out breath let the weight of the arm stretch your neck away from the wall. Always stretch on the out breath to avoid straining the muscle, and be careful not to pull too hard.

3. Turn your chin to look toward your outside armpit. Take a big breath in and then on your out breath, use the weight of the arm to pull the chin down to your chest, so that you can feel the stretch going up the back of your neck and down behind the shoulder blade.

4. Repeat on the other side.

thumbs up ~

A great stretch to release tension behind the shoulder blades and in the bra strap area, from carrying and bending with baby. Also great if you've slept in a funny position!

1. Semi-squat against the wall, suck your navel towards your spine and tilt the pelvis up so your lower back is flat against the wall.

2. Keep your shoulders and head against the wall, arms down by your side and thumbs pointing up.

3. Take in a big breath, and on the out breath, keeping your arms nice and straight, float your arms up to touch the wall behind you. Don't worry if you can't get all the way back, stop where you feel it straining.

4. Take a big breath in, navel to spine, and on the out breath, float the arms slowly down. The whole movement should be slow and controlled. Repeat 4–6 times.

Great for releasing tightness in hips, thighs and bottom, so it's perfect to do if you've been sitting for long periods of time with a hungry baby.

1. Sit on a chair with one foot on top of the opposite knee. Have your knee bent and your shin square in front of your body.

2. Sit up tall out of the pelvis and lean your body forward over the shin, until you feel the stretch in your hips, thighs and buttocks. Hold for 10 seconds and then release.

3. Repeat with the other leg.

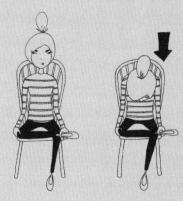

butt & leg ~

A fab stretch for the whole leg and bottom, especially if you suffered with pelvic girdle pain in pregnancy or have had stitches. It stretches into the bottom and hip, without opening up the pelvis or straining the sensitive groin area.

1. Stand with your body close to a table. Tuck the right foot tightly behind the left foot. With your hands on the table, tilt your tailbone up towards the ceiling.

2. Lower your chest towards the table, keep the tilt in the tailbone and push your bottom away from you. You should feel a stretch in the hamstring and bottom. Hold for 10 seconds.

3. Because you are working the right side, now twist the right hip over to the right, almost as if you are trying to touch it against the table. You should feel the stretch going down the leg and up into the hip and buttocks. Hold for 10 seconds.

4. Bring the hip back to the centre and slowly come back up to standing. Repeat on the left.

roll down ~

Brilliant for releasing the whole back and encouraging space between the vertebrae. Also great for the core.

1. Stand tall, chin tucked in. Pull your navel towards your spine, tuck your tail bone in and have your arms slightly in front and hands clasped together, palms facing down to the ground.

2. Reach your hands to the floor, as you roll down one vertebrae at a time. Stop when you feel your hamstrings pulling. Feel your shoulder blades open.

3. Once down, release the hands, take them behind your back and clasp them with palms facing up.

4. Take a big breath in, pull navel to spine and on the out breath reach your arms over your head.

5. Take a big breath in, pull navel to spine and on the out breath push your hands away from you as you roll up one vertebrae at a time, leaving your chin to come up last. Keep pushing your hands away, bringing them down towards your bottom. This will focus on the muscles behind the shoulder blades and allow them release.

6. Release your hands and feel the back and shoulder muscles loosen.

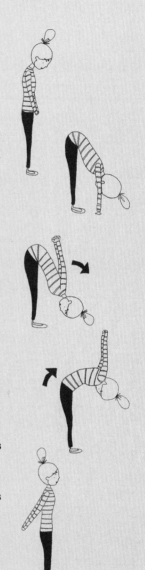

dive stretch ~

A wonderful stretch for when you feel tight in your ribs and the side of your tummy.

1. Take your arms up above your head and take hold of your right wrist with your left hand.

2. Take a big breath in and on the out breath stretch over to the left, pulling your right wrist over to the left.

3. Repeat on the other side, holding the left wrist with the right hand.

Healing Hands

Nearly all the new mums we work with postnatally complain of sore and achy bodies after birth. This isn't a surprise if we stop and consider what our body has been through. It has adapted over nine months to grow and house your little bean and then used every single muscle in labour to birth your baby. In its simplest form, labour is a series of muscle contractions and releases, often taking place over many hours. After a while, muscles can become fatigued and forget to fully release, leaving them in a contracted state and this is what causes a lot of the aches and pains.

If you have had a Caesarean you will undoubtedly have muscles that are sitting in contraction after being moved around during the abdominal birth of your little one, not to mention muscles that are now healing from the section site.

When you bring your baby home, your muscles continue to work hard. Carrying and feeding can put a real strain on your back and shoulders in those early weeks, as does the constant getting up in the night to tend to your baby's needs. It's no wonder that after a while you start to notice that your body feels uncomfortable.

In many cultures, massage plays a huge part in the care of a new mum, and is often carried out by the midwife herself – before, during and after labour. This shows a real understanding of the physical needs of the new mum and a focus on supporting and assisting her body to transition to its new postnatal state. It is not uncommon for women in these cultures to receive daily massages for thirty to forty days post birth! We know, right?! Why don't we do that?!?! Well, in some ways we can!

If finances allow, it's a great idea to see a trained professional after birth to give your body a once over and check your postnatal alignment. Lots of therapists will visit the house for postnatal visits, so you don't even have to get out of your pyjamas. Whether you see a professional or not, you can most definitely ask your partner to give you the odd shoulder rub or cheeky foot massage – ideally a couple of times a week for the first six weeks. If they complain, refer back to 'Understanding your Postnatal Body' on pages 17–21 and make them aware of all that your body is doing right now, and all that it has gone through, and how important it is that they support you!

Massaging a postnatal mum has so many benefits:

- **Muscle release:** Helps relieve stress left in the body after labour and releases tenseness caused by the mental and physical strain of caring for a newborn.

- **Oxytocin production:** Helps us feel happy, calm and cared for. Oxytocin also helps to stimulate milk flow.

- **Healing:** Encourages the body to heal and cells to renew.

- **Induces good sleep:** No explanation needed!

- **Stimulates the lymphatic system:** Improves wellbeing and strengthens the immune system. It also helps the body eliminate excess fluid and toxins, reducing fluid retention.

- **Regulates postpartum hormones:** Balances hormones and reduces the stress hormone cortisol.

- **Increases energy levels:** Encourages better circulation, helping us get rid of that sluggish feeling.

Massage: a wonderful breastfeeding support!

We once had a mum whose milk flow was very slow. She became incredibly tense, and baby would become very distressed at the breast and start flailing about and crying. We encouraged her partner to give her a massage at feed times. As mum sat feeding baby, we showed her partner how to do some light touch massage on her back (see page 56). She started to relax immediately, her shoulders softened and lowered, and as she relaxed, baby became calmer; before long we could hear baby swallowing milk happily. No more tears, and such a great flow of milk that the other breast started leaking too!

PLEASE NOTE:
Only massage on the muscle and never on the bone, as this is very sensitive, and can be painful. Do not massage over open wounds, or if mum is unwell or has a temperature.

partner massage

Light touch massage

Light touch massage is a gentle massage that can be done quickly and easily through clothing and in any situation. Sit in front of your partner so that your back is open to them, either on a stool, birthing ball or sit sideways on a chair.

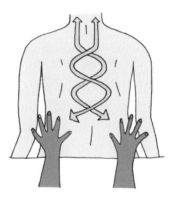

Instructions for your partner:

1. Sit facing your partner's back, and with the backs of your fingers, criss-cross your hands from the base of her spine to the top of her shoulders.

2. When you get to the shoulders, still using the backs of your fingers, stroke up her neck to the top of her head and back down again to her shoulders.

3. Criss-cross your hands back down to the base of the spine.

4. Repeat at least 5 times.

Deeper massage

Ask your partner to massage your muscles, but never on the bone. Start with a light pressure and build gradually if you desire. Make sure you are warm so you can fully relax and don't rush. Slow repetitive strokes are best for encouraging muscles to release and the body to drain itself of extra fluid.

The cradle hold (shiatsu)

This is a wonderful, easy shiatsu hold, designed for ultimate relaxation! Follow the instructions, then hold the position for 15–20 minutes (longer if you like!). This is great to do just before going to sleep, to allow your body to relax and let go of any stress or anxiety.

Instructions for your partner:

Sit behind mum, facing her back, while she is lying on her side. With your left hand, place the thumb into the occipital nook (the little ditch at the base of the skull) – the pressure should be minimal. Cradle the head with the rest of your hand. Be careful to keep the pressure as light as you can. Use the middle finger of your right hand to locate the coccyx (the end of the spine). Place the middle finger on the coccyx, fingers facing down towards the toes. The rest of the hand should cup the sacrum. Hold until your partner feels calm and sleepy. Be careful of your own posture in this position! Keep a straight back and use pillows to support your arms.

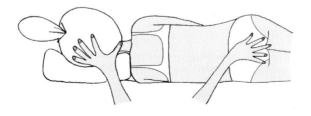

The back

The muscles on either side of the spine work hard in labour and during the postnatal period. Gentle massage up and down can be very soothing.

Instructions for your partner:

1. Starting at the sacrum towards the base of the spine, with a hand on either side of your partner's spine (never on it) massage up towards the head, over the shoulders and back down the sides.

2. Bring your hands back into the centre, on either side of the spine ready to repeat.

The shoulders

Ask your partner to massage your shoulders using their fingers and thumb, as though kneading bread. Then, with one hand on top of the other, start at the front edge of the shoulder, just above the shoulder blade, by the neck. Using the weight of both hands, trace the line of the shoulder blade down the back, out over the shoulder blade, up the outer edge of the shoulder and back to the starting position. Ask them to press down with as much pressure as you desire.

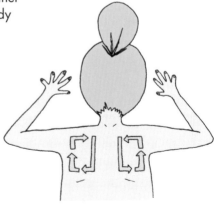

self massage

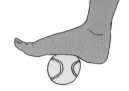

A wonderful way to get into tight spots by yourself is with a trusty tennis ball. Place the ball between you and the wall or the floor and use your body weight to provide pressure into the sore muscle. Hold the pressure into the muscle, and roll around the spot until you feel it release.

Bum muscles
Sandwich the ball between your bum muscle and the wall – use as much or as little pressure as you need. This is great for sciatic pain, or pinching in the bum muscle. It is great for women who have suffered with pelvic pain in pregnancy.

Neck and shoulders
Sandwich the ball between your shoulder muscles and the wall; again, lean into the ball for more pressure and ease off for less. Roll the ball around the muscle to release any tension.

Back
Lie on the ground and, using two tennis balls, place one either side of the spine (never on it) starting at the base. Lie back and allow your body to relax and feel the balls pressing into the tight muscles. Move the tennis balls up a bit and repeat. Keep moving them up, until they reach the shoulders.

Feet
It is not uncommon for the arches of our feet to tighten and flatten slightly in pregnancy and the early postnatal period. Place a tennis ball under the foot and roll your foot over the ball to release tension in the muscles that support the arch. Roll up and down and side to side. This is a good one to do while watching TV!

Nourishing Grub

We all know how important it is to eat well and to nourish our bodies, and this is especially important when we are healing after birth. Yet it is all too easy for a busy new mum to forget this or simply not have time to prepare food, living off cheese on toast and cake! Don't get us wrong, we love a bit of cheese on toast and cake, but we also know that eating well can make us feel better both physically and mentally, and will help our body to recover from birth more quickly.

In many cultures all over the world, food plays a huge part in the postnatal care of new mums. We know that a mum eating healthily will feel less worn out and more able to feed and nurture her baby. In our experience of working with new mums in the UK, however, it's apparent just how little most women understand about what their body really needs in the early postnatal weeks, so we've listed the main nutrients we need to help our body do its postnatal thing! We would encourage women to eat as wide a range of food as possible to ensure all nutrients are covered, but see our list for some advice on what foods contain which nutrients.

CALCIUM

Not only great for healthy bones, calcium helps blood to clot and muscles to contract, aiding postnatal healing. Find it in dairy products, dark green leafy veg, sardines, almonds and fortified cereals.

FIBRE

Very important to combat postnatal constipation, so eat plenty of fresh fruit and veg, lentils and wholegrain cereals.

IRON

It's not at all uncommon for a new mum to feel tired, forgetful and confused. Mostly this is down to lack of sleep, but it can be a sign of an iron deficiency. Iron-rich foods include meat, fish, green leafy veg, kidney beans, prunes, apricots and baked potatoes with the skin on. Powdered spirulina is a great iron supplement you can add to smoothies or yoghurts. If you are concerned your iron is low, get it checked by your GP.

MAGNESIUM

Helps ease cramps and restless legs and balances moods. Magnesium can be a great help for anxiety and PMS-type symptoms too, which can arise after birth due to hormonal imbalances. It also works with calcium and vitamin D to keep our bones healthy. Eat plenty of spinach, fish, almonds, tofu, cashews, black beans, brown rice and oats.

OMEGA-3 FATTY ACIDS

Support the nervous system, improve sleep, promote a healthy heart, reduce inflammation and essential for good skin health and healthy hormone balance! Found in oily fish, such as mackerel, salmon and sardines (but stick to 2 or 3 portions a week), as well as walnuts, chia seeds and flaxseeds.

POTASSIUM

Essential for good cell function, helping nutrients move in and waste products move out. Maintains fluid balance and aids metabolism and energy levels. Fruit and veg are the best sources, particularly watercress, parsley and celery.

PROTEIN

Helps repair muscle and other tissues to keep your body strong. It also helps keep your energy up. Eat lean meats, beans, fish, eggs and soy products.

SELENIUM

Has antioxidant properties that can help protect against free radicals, reduce inflammation, enhance the immune system and support energy levels. Find it in tuna, salmon, beef, mushrooms, cheese and Brazil nuts.

VITAMIN A
Important for skin health and wound healing, and also enhances immunity. Eat red and orange fruit and veg, such as sweet potato, butternut squash, carrots, watermelon and tomatoes. Green leafy veg, milk and eggs are also great sources.

VITAMIN B
The vitamin B family are great for lifting your mood and helping to fight fatigue. Eat more lentils, beans and wholegrain breakfast cereals.

VITAMIN C
New mums need lots of vitamin C. It helps with healing and keeps the immune system strong. Eat oranges, green leafy veg, peppers, berries, kiwi fruit, tomatoes and peas.

VITAMIN D
Essential for maintaining a strong immune system and for regulating hormones. It also helps your body absorb calcium properly. The best food sources are salmon, cheese and eggs. Or take your baby out for a walk in the sunshine!

VITAMIN E
Great for your immune system and a healthy heart. Also aids skin repair/healing. For breastfeeding mums, vitamin E is especially important as baby needs it to help fight against anaemia and boost the immune system. Find it in sunflower seeds, almonds, peanut butter, toasted wheatgerm, avocado and cooked brown rice.

VITAMIN K
Controls blood clotting and is also important for bone health as it ensures our body uses calcium effectively. Green leafy veg are very high in this vitamin, particularly broccoli, watercress and cabbage. Potatoes, tomatoes and milk are also good sources.

ZINC
A true wonder mineral. Essential for good healing and boosting your immune health. Also supports healthy skin and hormone balance, helps us cope with stress and helps maintain energy levels. Beef and lamb, pumpkin seeds and ginger are some of the best sources.

Keep your fluids up

We lose a lot of body fluid in the early postnatal period from blood loss, hormone sweats and milk production, so it is important to keep hydrated. We tend to get very thirsty in those initial weeks! Create a feeding nook in the house and keep a big bottle of water, snacks and a good book there – that way, when you sit down to feed baby, you'll have everything you need at your fingertips. No more settling down to feed only to realise you've forgotten a glass of water! Keeping up your fluids also helps with hormonal headaches, insomnia, tiredness and constipation. Try to drink at least 8–10 glasses a day or more if your thirst requires.

Top tips for eating better

1. Friends and family love to help out, so ask them for a big cheesy lasagne or some pasta sauces or tasty soups that you can freeze. Or if they're not really the cooking type, ask them to pick up a few ready meals to have on standby – just aim for healthy ones and with low salt.

2. Eat little and often. Let's face it, routines are all over the place in the early days and probably so are your meal times. Hormonal changes, tiredness and the healing body all mean new mums can feel hungrier than usual. Snacking is also a great opportunity to get in some extra nutrients. Eating regularly will also help keep blood sugar levels stable – low blood sugar can make us feel emotionally wobbly and anxious. Have a few healthy snacks at the ready to stop you reaching for the digestives. There's nothing wrong with the odd sweet

treat, but try to avoid the dreaded sugar rollercoaster by opting for more natural alternatives. See pages 72–73 for our favourite snack ideas. You need an extra 500 or so calories a day if you're breastfeeding, but just listen to your body and eat when you are hungry.

3. When your partner gets back from work or when baby is having a snooze, do a little bit of food prep. Spending time bonding with your baby or having a bath or a nap is far more important than spending hours batch cooking in the kitchen, but chopping up some veggies and shoving them in an airtight box in the fridge means you'll have something fresh to snack on with your hummus.

4. Overnight oats were a complete game-changer for us. They are so easy to make and you will have a healthy breakfast (or anytime snack) ready to go. See the recipe on page 68.

5. Having pre-prepared smoothie packs in the freezer ensures you have a nutrient boost to hand whenever you are hungry or having an energy dip – just pop the frozen fruit and veg in the blender with some milk or coconut water and blitz! See our recipes on pages 66–67.

6. Get an online food delivery each week so your cupboards and fridge always contain something healthy and quick to eat. Stock up on avocados, celery sticks, spinach, eggs, oatcakes, rice cakes, hummus, cheese, bananas, apples, cucumber, carrots, nut butters and quick-cook rice and couscous. Keep some bread, bagels, milk, salmon steaks and healthy ready meals in the freezer for emergencies.

7. Soups are a great quick lunch and will keep in the fridge for a couple of days. Freeze some nice bread too, so you can make toast whenever you want, without the risk of it going stale (make sure it is sliced before you freeze it!).

Anything to avoid?

Most mums will find they can eat what they like with no trouble at all. Some babies, though, can be a little sensitive to certain foods that can pass into the breast milk.

Things you may want to keep an eye on are:

- Spices: some babies can be unsettled by garlic and chilli.

- Gassy veggies: a windy baby is no fun! Be careful with veg such as onion, cabbage, cauliflower and broccoli.

- Tea, coffee and alcohol: limit yourself to one or two cups of tea or coffee a day as too much caffeine can interfere with your baby's sleep and mood. The same goes for alcohol – the occasional glass is fine, but more than one drink and the alcohol will enter your milk.

Okay — now for the best bit: a great all-rounder for a new mum is... dark CHOCOLATE! High in minerals such as iron, magnesium, copper, zinc, selenium and potassium, it's a great pick-me-up to combat new-mum tiredness. Don't eat too much, though, especially if you are breastfeeding late at night, as it does have a small amount of naturally occurring caffeine.

recipes ~ smoothies

Make mine a smoothie ···

We often suggest to partners that every morning, they make their ladies a pint of smoothie before doing anything else! This way, even if you don't manage to eat anything other than toast for the rest of the day, you'll have had a vitamin injection to fuel you! Invest in a good blender that is easy to clean.

Chop all your fruit in one go and freeze in individual smoothie portions – label your portions so you know what's inside! Then just grab a bag from the freezer and tip it straight into the blender with water, milk or a dairy-free milk (we like coconut and oat milks). You can also buy bags of frozen fruit from the supermarket, which are usually cheaper than fresh.

Below are our favourite recipes for new mums. Add all the ingredients to a blender and whizz until smooth, adding more liquid if it's too thick, and a few ice cubes if you'd like it chilled.

Each makes roughly 550ml

Iron boosting
a handful of spinach
½ avocado
a handful of kale
a small handful of blueberries
a small bunch of mint leaves
1 tablespoon flaxseeds
1 tablespoon chia seeds
250ml water
3 dried apricots
3 dates, stones removed

Constipation easing
5 prunes, stones removed
5 dates, stones removed
250ml organic apple juice
250ml milk or dairy-free milk
280g organic natural yoghurt
½ teaspoon cinnamon
a pinch of nutmeg

Energising

3 dates, stones removed
½ avocado
½ banana
2 tablespoons chia seeds
½ orange
225g pineapple chunks
225g strawberries
½ pear, peeled
a handful of spinach
250ml milk or dairy-free milk

Diuretic

250ml organic apple juice
225g pineapple chunks
a handful of watercress
1 celery stick
a handful of grapes
a handful of blueberries

Stomach settling

½ avocado
½ banana
225g pineapple chunks
225g melon chunks
1 celery stick
1 teaspoon chopped fresh ginger
2 tablespoons chia seeds
250ml organic apple juice
½ teaspoon turmeric
2 tablespoons organic
   natural yoghurt

Immune boosting

a small handful of roughly
   chopped kale
a small handful of spinach
225g pineapple chunks
225g chopped kiwi
120g blackberries
½ avocado
1 tablespoon peanut butter
1 teaspoon elderberry extract
   (great if you have it, but
   don't worry if not)
1 tablespoon honey
120g chopped mango
½ teaspoon grated ginger
½ teaspoon cinnamon
½ teaspoon ground
   cardamom
250ml milk or dairy-free milk

Breastfeeding buddy

1 banana
120g oats
2 tablespoons peanut butter
1 tablespoon brewer's yeast
2 tablespoons cacao powder
1 teaspoon vanilla extract
1 tablespoon milled flaxseed
1 tablespoon maple syrup
250ml milk or coconut milk

recipes ~ breakfast

Mornings can be a bit unruly so make this the night before.

Overnight oats ···

A firm favourite of ours, overnight oats are a great way to ensure you have a filling breakfast (perfect if you have kids to get ready for school too) and can also be eaten as a snack throughout the day for a bit of an energy boost. Oats are great for slow-release energy to keep you going and fab for breastfeeding mums to help keep milk supply tip-top. They are also high in fibre so can help prevent or ease constipation.

Serves 1

20g oats
125ml milk of your choice
2 tablespoons organic
   natural yogurt

Mix all the ingredients together in a small bowl.

Stir in your chosen flavours (see our suggestions below) and leave in the fridge overnight.

The oats can be eaten cold in the morning or heated in the microwave or in a small pan for a warming porridge.

Optional flavour add-ins:

- Chopped fruit
- Dollop of nut butter
- Honey
- Cinnamon
- Mixed seeds, e.g. sunflower, chia, poppy, linseed, pumpkin
- Ground ginger
- Ground nutmeg
- Dried fruit, e.g. dates, prunes, apricots, goji berries and raisins – dried fruit does contain a lot of natural sugars, so be careful how much you have
- Coconut flakes
- Chia seeds
- Dark chocolate chips – but don't overdo it!

recipes ~ lunch

If you can eat lunch one-handed then so much the better!

Easy chicken noodle soup ···

This is a delicious soup you can feel working wonders even as you eat it! Make a big batch and eat it over a few days or freeze the extra. Defrost fully before reheating thoroughly.

For the broth (serves 4–6)

1 whole chicken
2 celery sticks
2 carrots
1 onion or leek
1 bay leaf
a pinch of peppercorns

For the soup (serves 1)

a large handful of seasonal
    veg, e.g. kale, spinach,
    mini sweetcorn (halved),
    chopped carrots, green beans
a handful of cooked chicken
1 x portion of noodles
crusty bread, to serve

First make the broth. Place the whole chicken in a big pan with the rest of the broth ingredients. Cover with water and bring to the boil, then reduce the heat and simmer for 1–1½ hours. Top up with more water if needed.

Remove the chicken and leave to cool. Remove the meat and return the bones to the broth. Simmer gently for 30 minutes.

Strain the broth into a clean pan and separate into portions. Leave one portion in the pan and store the rest in the freezer or fridge (it will keep for up to 6 months in the freezer and a couple of days in the fridge).

To make up your soup, add the veg to the broth. Bring to the boil, then add the cooked chicken and noodles. Simmer until the noodles are cooked. Serve with crusty bread.

recipes ~ dinner

Eat this in your PJs on the sofa in front of the TV!

Sweet potato shepherd's pie ···

You can batch cook this and freeze in portions. Once frozen, defrost thoroughly and cook in the oven for 20–30 minutes until hot all the way through. Serve with green veg or a green salad.

Serves 4

1 tablespoon olive oil
2 celery sticks, finely chopped
2 carrots, peeled and
  finely chopped
1 onion, finely chopped
500g beef mince
2 tablespoons tomato purée
1 x 400g tin tomatoes
1 teaspoon dried mixed herbs
50g frozen peas
600g sweet potato, peeled
  and chopped
60ml milk
20g butter
35g grated cheddar cheese
salt and pepper, to season

Heat the oil in large pan over a medium heat and cook the celery, carrots and onions for 3–4 minutes, or until the onion has softened. Add the mince, stirring with a wooden spoon to break up any clumps. Cook for 5 minutes until browned.

Add the tomato purée, tinned tomatoes and dried herbs. When it starts to bubble, reduce the heat and simmer for 20–25 minutes until thickened. Stir in the peas.

Preheat the oven to 180°C/160°C fan. Boil the sweet potatoes in a pan for 8 minutes, or until just tender. Drain and return to the pan. Add the milk and butter and mash until smooth.

Spoon the beef into an oven dish about 5cm deep. (Or divide into two smaller baking dishes – one for the freezer and one for the oven!) Top with the potato and cheese. Bake for 30–35 minutes until golden.

recipes ~ sweet treats

Better than a biscuit!

Energy balls ···

These are an easy, tasty alternative to bought cakes and treats. Experiment with different flavours – try adding a handful of chopped almonds, a tablespoon or two of cacao powder, a tablespoon of desiccated coconut, a few chopped dried apricots or a small handful of raisins.

Makes about 10

2 handfuls of dates,
  stones removed
3 tablespoons milled flaxseed
3 tablespoons oats
a handful of almonds
2 tablespoons coconut oil
(solid or liquid is fine)
3 tablespoons nut butter
2 tablespoons honey

Blitz all the ingredients together in a food processor; the mixture should be nice and sticky.

Roll into bite-sized balls, place on a tray and pop in the fridge for a couple of hours to set.

Scoff whenever you feel the need for a sweet pick-me-up!

easy snacks + quick meals

Avocado on toast
Everyone's at it! Smashed avo on toast is very trendy these days, and for good reason. This amazing superfood is full of so much goodness. Add banana or honey for a creamy sweet snack or feta or a poached egg for a protein hit.

Banana bites
Cut a banana into bite-sized chunks, put a teaspoon of nut butter on top of each chunk and finish with a sprinkling of dark chocolate chips and a pinch of sea salt. A perfect, moreish quick fix.

Apple and nut butter
Slice your apple, dollop some nut butter into a bowl and use it as a dip for the apple.

Cream cheese on celery sticks
Celery is full of goodness, and because of its unique shape it's also great to fill with a yummy dip! Nut butter also works well.

That's a wrap
Dollop on some hummus, guacamole or salsa, bung in a handful of spinach salad or some veg, such as chopped red pepper, add a chopped hard-boiled egg, some grated cheese or cooked chicken, roll it up and scoff. For a sweet wrap, fill with yoghurt, honey, raisins, chocolate chips or chopped fruit.

Quick salads
- Chop up mozzarella, tomato and avocado for the quickest, yummiest tricolour salad.
- Chop up some watermelon (or buy a pack of watermelon cubes) and mix with feta cheese and mint for a more exotic salad fix.
- Toss together cashews, spring onions and beansprouts with a splash of soy sauce for a bit of a change.
- Leftover boiled or roasted potatoes are great with tuna, black olives and cucumber for a tasty, filling salad for those hungrier moments.

Beans and cheese on toast
This classic is full of fibre and calcium, and it really hits the spot on those tired, 'I need stodge' kind of days! Add Marmite to the toast for a little kick, or a fried egg for some extra-filling protein.

The loyal jacket potato
High in fibre, vitamin C and B vitamins (especially B6), they are tasty, filling and nutritious. Use a regular baking potato or sweet potato. Sweet potatoes are high in vitamins A, B5, B6, B1, B3, B2 and carotenoids.

Serves 1

Scrub your spud, pierce the skin and brush with oil. Place on a baking tray and scatter with salt. Bake for 1 hour, or until soft when poked with a knife. (Or microwave for about 10 minutes.) Slice it open, add a knob of butter to the fluffy inside and top with a tasty filling. This is where you can get your vitamin fix – think about what you might be needing and go wild...

- Cheese and beans – protein, calcium and fibre
- Tuna and sweetcorn with mayo – protein, omega 3 and vitamin C
- Cottage cheese, bacon and avocado – protein, calcium, vitamin K and vitamin E
- Hummus, cherry tomatoes, black olives and baby spinach – protein, magnesium, vitamin C, iron

Granola pot
Bung some shop-bought granola into a bowl with a dollop of yoghurt or a splash of milk, some chopped banana or a handful or raspberries, a squeeze of honey and hey presto: a lovely filling granola pot! Opt for a low-sugar variety as granola can be high in sugar.

Bulk up your soup
When you are tired and hungry, sometimes soup just isn't filling enough. Add some microwaved or pre-cooked rice to the soup to bulk it up and make it into a more substantial meal.

a nice cup of tea

Nothing is more comforting than a steaming mug of soothing tea (and, even better, if someone makes it for you!). The tradition of drinking herbal teas has been passed down through the generations for centuries. They can support a woman in both mind and body as she adjusts to motherhood, and can really help you feel warm and supported from the inside out. Herbal teas are also a great way to stay hydrated, help flush out toxins (especially if you had an epidural or meds during the birth) and are a great caffeine-free alternative to tea and coffee. The teas we have listed below are available from most health food shops on the high street and online, and are recommended to us by Jo Farren – a medical herbalist who works a lot with new mums.

If you're using loose-leaf tea, start off with 1 heaped teaspoon per cup of hot water and adjust to taste. If you're using bags, cover the top of the cup while it steeps for 10–15 minutes to keep it warm. While you wait, have a quick stretch (see page 46), take some deep breaths, and try to take a moment to focus on yourself. Add a little honey to your brewed tea if you like, curl up on the sofa and revel in the joy of drinking a HOT cuppa, which in busy all-consuming mum life is a win in itself!

Teas for detoxifying and hormone balancing

Dandelion
Dandelion leaf is a wonderful source of flavonoids and potassium and acts as a diuretic, supporting the kidneys. The root has a supporting effect on the liver, helping the body to break down toxins and expel waste.

Nettle leaf
A good source of iron, calcium, vitamin K and potassium, this wonderful herb helps to nourish the new mother. As it has a gentle diuretic effect, it's great for water retention and helps to flush out toxins.

Teas to calm and soothe

Chamomile
High in calcium and magnesium and commonly used to help with anxiety and sleeplessness, as well as calming and soothing digestion. We also use it in our soothing breast and perineal pads! (See pages 35 and 40.)

Withania Ashwagandha
Also known as Indian Ginseng, this is a wonderful adaptogenic herb (meaning it stabilises the systems of the body), thought to be relaxing while preserving energy and improving stamina. A really useful adrenal tonic, perfect for 'tired and wired' mothers.

Teas for energy and physical healing

Alfalfa
High in vitamin K and essential minerals which may help prevent postpartum haemorrhage from occurring. A great all-rounder as it is packed full of an array of vitamins and minerals.

Spearmint leaf
Can help with digestion and upset stomach, nausea, gas and bloating. Great for C-section mamas to drink after surgery to ease symptoms of trapped wind.

Teas to encourage milk supply

Aim to drink 4–6 cups daily. Please note though that the most important factor in breastfeeding is attachment. (See pages 40–43 and 162–165 for more on breastfeeding and support.)

Holy thistle (blessed thistle)
Can help increase breast milk supply and it also has a protective effect on the liver and digestive system.

Raspberry leaf
As well as helping to tone the uterus, this herb can improve the flow of milk.

Space to heal

As soon as the news breaks that your little person has arrived, you are likely to be inundated with calls, messages and emails from well-wishers who want to book in for a cuddle and a cuppa. There is something so special about introducing your baby to everyone. Your pride will be overflowing and you will want to share the love! However, it is very important for you and your partner to ease yourselves gently into parenthood without having to entertain queues of visitors.

In the early days and weeks after giving birth, be honest with family and friends about your need to rest and get to know your baby. It is not self-indulgent or bad manners; it is essential as you start on your motherhood journey. Never feel guilty about following your body's natural cues – they are letting you know what you need. Take it slowly and be gentle with yourself as you heal. There will be plenty of time for rounds of tea and cake in the weeks and months to come!

We are lucky in the UK that we have two weeks' statutory paternity leave so partners can take time out to adjust to parenthood themselves and support mum. This time away from the demands of working life is so valuable for both of you. There is a reason why this time is offered as paternity leave. It is NOT time off to rearrange a vinyl collection into alphabetical order, paint the decking or clean out the attic. It is time to spend adapting to your new life as parents, resting where possible, bonding with your baby and supporting one another. If you already have children, then your partner is likely to be busy looking after them too so that mum can concentrate on meeting the needs of baby. Maybe explain to people that while you can't wait to show off your gorgeous baby, you will need the company more once your partner's leave is up, and that it would mean the world to you if they could book in for this time.

You will no doubt have some visitors in the first few weeks though, and one of your partner's jobs can be to organise the diary and space out the amount of people who are coming to meet baby. We feel that the best times for visitors is mid-morning or mid-afternoon. That way you don't have to rush out of bed in the morning to meet and greet them – there are few things a midwife likes to see more than a couple still in their jammies at 10am snuggled up and having a love-in with their new baby – lush! Your visitors also won't be around in the evening when you're getting hungry/want to have a sleep before the night feeds commence.

And remember, they are visitors not guests. Your role is not to host for friends and family during this time so don't be afraid to ask your visitors to help out where you need it – maybe picking up a pint of milk or bringing over something for dinner on their way round. It is such an honour to support and nurture a new mum and it can make visitors feel like they are really able to help as you adapt to parenthood in those initial hazy days. We also urge that you let guests know when you are starting to feel tired and want to take to your bed for a little rest, especially if your baby is having a kip. If you worry that this is not polite, just consider for a moment who exactly is going to be up with baby at 3am changing, feeding and settling them, and let go of any guilt you have!

SAY YES!

When a new mum is asked if she needs anything, often the automatic response is 'No thank you, we're good'. This comes partly from being polite, and partly from not having the brain power to actually think of what you might need at that precise moment! You don't need to be polite! Your friends and family will love having a job to do for you. Often friends and family really want to help, but they might not know what you need, so asking directly is much easier all round. Keep a list on your phone of the things you need on a day-to-day basis. Every time you are running low on something, add it to the list. The next time you are asked the question 'Do you need anything?' you'll be able to check your list, and without racking your tired brain, you'll be able to say yes! And if in doubt, ask for food!

Suggestions include:

- Bring over hearty food such as lasagne, shepherd's pie, soups, casseroles and, of course, cake!

- Do a bit of washing up or stack/unstack the dishwasher.

- Put a wash on, hang it out, or perhaps fold up some laundry.

- Run the hoover over the floors.

- Watch baby while you have a bath or shower or take a nap. Your guests will love the 'cuddle time'!

- Post thank you letters.

- Read a magazine or newspaper to you while you feed so you can feel connected to the world outside.

- Pop to the shops to buy you anything you need — nappies, pads, wipes, snacks to stock up the cupboard.

- Take your older kids to the park for an hour or two.

minding

a mother

As your body heals from birthing your baby, your mind will also be adapting to the incredible changes that have taken place. You'll be facing so many new emotions as you experience all the joys and challenges a baby brings to your life.

The first weeks and months of new parenthood can feel like a huge adjustment period – to say the very least. It's especially important during this time to avoid falling into the trap of parenthood perfectionism. Be kind and gentle with your body and mind as you evolve into a brand-new, enriched version of yourself.

Enjoy your slow days when they happen, stay in your PJs, snuggle with your baby and potter around the house. These days can be so restorative and healing but, remember, if your mood drops or you are having a day where it all feels like too much of a struggle, reach out and bring in the tribe – you'll be amazed how much of a tonic a cuppa and a chat about it all can be.

Know also that this time will pass. So don't sweat the small stuff. No one loves to be surrounded by piles of messy laundry, dirty mugs and general mayhem when their home, and life, once felt calm and relaxed. But give yourself some time

and soon you will adjust to a new normal and start to feel more in control of your surroundings again. For now, though, don't worry about a bit of mess! Spend the time resting and bonding with your baby instead.

Acknowledge how you feel, whether it be a light or dark mood, and do not judge or beat yourself up if life feels chaotic at present. Nothing is constant. Life has seasons and is constantly changing. Although this is good to remember when things are a bit tough, make time to appreciate all the good moments too.

Finally, it's really important to remember you don't have to do it all alone. We know it sounds a bit cheesy, but we genuinely are stronger together!

No Comparisons

While you heal from the incredible work your body has done, we urge you to take your time and go at your own pace. As hard as it may feel, try not to compare yourself with how well other people APPEAR to be doing. You don't necessarily know what is going on, no matter how quickly they seem to be fitting back into their pre-pregnancy jeans, hitting the park for a run with their jogging buggy or how calm they seem in their smiley selfies with their baby on Instagram.

It tends to be when you are feeling most exhausted and vulnerable that everyone else seems to be having the best time. Looking at other mothers' postnatal journeys and convincing yourself that they are doing a better job than you, that they are having more fun with their baby or that their baby is more easy-going then yours can feel soul destroying. In reality, every new mum is adjusting to parenthood. We are all different and it isn't helpful to look at others and wonder why we seem to be finding it so much harder, berating ourselves for being unwashed at midday and struggling to make it to the local shop for a pint of milk. Having a new baby is a huge adjustment and on some level they will be feeling it too, whether they are showing it to the world or not.

We seem to have lost something in our Western culture around honouring recovery post birth. We get caught up in silly 'bounce back' timings which can lead to exhaustion and troubling mental health. Expecting a woman to ping back to her pre-pregnant self in a swift six weeks is ridiculous. Even if you feel well and your body appears to be returning to the way it looked prior to pregnancy, your hormones are likely to still be unbalanced and your mind will still be adjusting to this significant life change. Don't compare yourself with anyone. Do things in your own sweet time.

'I once opened the door to the postman just as my friend was arriving. As I did, the dog escaped and my baby did a loud 'up the backer' nappy. As I took the parcel off the postman, while shouting madly at the dog, I saw my hand and sleeve were covered in baby poo. Meanwhile, my friend gave me a strange nod and I looked down to see my top hooked up, with nipple out post-feed, blinding the postman. Just then my friend's baby sicked up all over her hair and down her top. We high-fived and doubled over laughing while the postman tried awkwardly to catch the dog. It's been an absolute lifesaver to laugh through the chaos with other mums who are totally in it with you!'

~ Helena, mum of three

Getting Out There

Spending time with other people can make us feel so much better. We can get fooled into thinking that scrolling through social media gives us our fill of social interaction but the simple fact is that there is nothing quite like face-to-face human contact. When you feel ready, planning a few things in your maternity leave that will get you out of the house and enjoying the company of others can lift your spirits greatly.

- Meet with your antenatal group for a walk with buggies around the park.

- Join a local singing/dancing/baby massage class.

- Go to a mum-and-baby cinema screening with a friend.

- Attend a postnatal Pilates, yoga or BuggyFit class.

- Arrange a picnic at a local park with friends (weather permitting!).

- Start or join a regular coffee morning with other mums on maternity leave. The host provides the drinks and the guests provide the nibbles.

- Arrange to meet up with work friends or friends without children and have some time out from talking about motherhood and a mini-break from conversations about baby poo and sleep (or lack of it).

Love Your Love Lines

After you have birthed your baby, your body starts changing all over again. Breasts get ready to offer up a food source and fill up with milk, growing bigger and more veiny (think Hulk boobs), and your tummy, once hard and full of a baby, now feels empty and wobbly. And all over again you will find yourself needing to adjust to these changes, this time getting used to your new postnatal body.

Just as pregnancy bumps come in all different sizes, so too will your postnatal body be unique to you. Everybody will have their own personal journey. Your body will change in a way that is perfect for you but may be very different to your best friend or to the women at your mum and baby group. We've seen oodles of milk from small breasts and big breasts with a smaller milk supply. Bumps and hips will shrink back differently from woman to woman, some will be left with ribs that stick out more than they used to, while others will have patchy skin from postnatal hormones. Your body is changing, and it will do it in its own time and in its own way.

While training with Mexican midwives, Beccy remembers being taken aback by a conversation that happened during class. The teaching midwife kept referring to 'love lines', and after a while a midwife from the UK asked her what she meant by this. The Mexican midwife looked confused, as if she couldn't quite believe they didn't know what she was talking about. She explained what she meant and then asked what we called them in the UK. The UK midwife explained that in the West they were called 'stretch marks'. The Mexican midwife looked disgusted: 'Such ugly language,' she said, and continued with her teaching. Later that day, the class were talking about blocks to maternal mental wellbeing, and another birth professional discussed the pressure on women to diet and exercise, often before their bodies are ready, in order to 'get back to their pre-baby body'. Another student joined in saying that a lot of her ladies didn't want a 'mum body' and she associated being a mum with negative body image. Again, the Mexican midwife shook her head and looked puzzled. 'Your body is different now, it has changed for ever, why do you want it to be like it was before, why not like it now?'

This story made us think a lot about our societal expectations to 'bounce back', 'carry on as normal' and 'not let the baby change you'. The language used around motherhood is often quite negative: 'Oh, she's still got her baby weight' or 'She's a bit mumsy' are sentences we hear often. But why do we not embrace the postnatal period as other cultures do? Why do we not reassure new mums that their bodies are beautiful and functioning perfectly, just as they should? Our postnatal bodies are amazing and we should respect them and cherish them for the awesome job they have done, and are continuing to do.

Remember that after giving birth your body stores fat as an energy reserve for milk production, and that you have high levels of relaxin, a hormone that allowed your muscles to stretch to accommodate and give birth to your baby. This hormone also means that your muscles will be a little looser after the birth. It won't always be this way, but right now your body is more concerned with feeding that baby than getting back into skinny jeans. Follow its lead, it's smarter than you think!

Imagine if we grew up in a society where stretch marks were called love lines and we were taught to look forward to our new body with all its changes. Would we find it easier to love ourselves a little more? After all, we've created life: our body grew a human and then birthed it. Now our body continues to care for and nurture baby on the outside. Surely that deserves love and celebration and not criticism?

Ways to love your postnatal body

- **Look at yourself:** Think about all that your body has done, and celebrate that! Your body is truly amazing. It grew and birthed a baby (however your birth played out). Take some time to look at yourself in the mirror and acknowledge each and every part that has enabled you to become a mother. The love lines that may be peppered across your body, the postnatal tummy, perhaps the C-section line. Every single change, however small, is evidence of the miraculous experience that you have been through, and are still going through.

- **Forgive your body:** If birth did not play out as you had hoped because your baby wasn't in the right position, had managed to get a little wedged in there or perhaps was getting tired and distressed and needed a helping hand being born, then it's important to understand that there really wasn't anything your body could have done to change your birthing story. It did the best it could do under the circumstances. Make peace with it and celebrate the incredible achievement of creating another human from scratch.

- **Nourish your skin:** Rather than focusing on any lumps or bumps and wasting negative energy on being self-deprecating about your body, nourish and nurture yourself from top to bottom. Bathe, exfoliate, pop on a calming or refreshing facemask or eye mask and apply your favourite lotions and potions that feel deliciously soft and nourishing for your skin. Giving yourself a once-over occasionally can feel wonderfully nurturing and really is a little act of self-love for that body of yours.

- **Cosy up:** During the postnatal period your body often feels vulnerable and highly sensitive. Treat yourself to a super-cosy, soft item of clothing that does not feel uncomfortable or restrictive against your body and enjoy being at ease. Leave those pre-pregnancy clothes to one side for now and enjoy comfort over aesthetics.

- **Rest:** When we are tired it can be hard to feel positive and it's all too easy to start picking fault with ourselves. Instead of getting into a negative mindset, try and get some healing and restorative rest where possible and you will ALWAYS feel better for it (see 'The Importance of Rest, Part 1' on page 29 and 'The Importance of Rest, Part 2' on page 154).

- **Move:** You may feel a little slower than usual in the weeks that follow birth. Be aware of how each part of you is feeling and be careful not to overdo it, especially if you have had any complications, stitches or a C-section. Remember to be very careful with yourself, particularly in those initial six weeks. When you feel able to, follow our simple postnatal yoga sequence on pages 174–177 or incorporate some of our postnatal stretches into your day wherever possible (see pages 46–52). It may help remind you of how energising it can feel to get yourself moving once again.

- **Eat well:** We absolutely understand how easy it is to reach for sugary foods when you are tired and short of time. We have been there ourselves. But you can't live on tea and biscuits alone as it won't make you feel good – physically or mentally. Most new mums seem to have a much sweeter tooth after baby is born, so make some naturally sweet and nutritious energy snacks. See our recipe for Energy Balls on page 71.

Community

We were never meant to parent in isolation, and having family and friends around us is invaluable, especially in the early days. If you look at mothers in tribal or village communities in Africa, Asia, South America and the Middle East, they often share the workload of raising a child, living close to each other, caring for each other and, in some places, feeding each other's children. In these communities, women tend to feel more supported and safe. They often feel less anxious, less isolated, less sleep-deprived and find breastfeeding easier. There are also fewer reported cases of postnatal depression. It takes a village to raise a child!

Historically, childbirth and motherhood are closely associated with long-standing traditions and rituals. It was through the passing on of these customs and beliefs that knowledge and understanding of birth and motherhood was shared from generation to generation. In Nigeria, the tradition of *omugwo*, which means 'postnatal care', is practised, which is a lovely tradition whereby the grandmother gives baby its first bath. If the grandmother isn't around, this is done by another female relative, and it's a symbol to the mother that she isn't alone and that her female community are there for her.

Learning to adjust to motherhood can be a wobbly ride, and it really does help to have others by your side to share the worries, the joys and the workload. These days, busy work schedules and families living further apart from each other mean that it can be harder to support a new mum in this practical way. Opposite are some ways to help you feel connected to those closest to you, even if they don't live around the corner.

Keeping in touch with family and friends

- **Set up a message group:** Post pictures and share stories as the days and weeks go past so that family and friends can be with you on your parenthood journey.

- **Schedule keeping in touch:** Have a regular day and time when you get in touch via a video or phone call.

- **Send out actual photos:** Many companies online can now turn your phone photos into cards, postcards or fridge magnets in just a few clicks. It's so easy to do and a lovely way to share your motherhood journey while giving your granny something to keep and treasure.

- **Social media:** Although it's not always a good thing, social media can be a wonderful way to keep up to date with those you care about most. When you get round to seeing your old friend that lives halfway across the country, you still know what they have been up to. However, remember we often show the best bits on social media so be careful not to assume that someone else's life is perfect just because that's what the pictures suggest.

- **Plan a visit:** As wonderful and useful as other ways of keeping in touch are nothing beats seeing each other face-to-face and spending quality time together. Get the diary out and book them in. Make sure that you have one or two scheduled visits from friends and family every week. Mentally it will really help to know that you have company booked in to break up the days, and a spare pair of hands if needed. Staggering those early visits will really come into its own and you will be so glad you paced the flow of guests.

A mother warming

More and more of our new mums are having a postnatal 'mother blessing' or 'mother warming'. This is a celebration to honour and care for the new mother and is organised by her closest friends – a little like a hen party but without the alcohol and naughty straws. The celebration is focused on showing the new mother that she is surrounded by friends who want to help and support her. Food and beverages are brought to the new mum's house and a lovely spread is set out. Maybe someone will give mum a massage, or do her nails for her, or perhaps everyone will just generally pamper her for the day, while helping her with the baby. Friends will also often bring gifts for the mum that are focused around healing her mind and body. Typical gifts include herbal teas, candles, body lotions, books, clothes, a pick-me-up jar (see below) or anything that will make the new mum feel pampered and celebrated.

A 'PICK-ME-UP' JAR

A 'pick-me-up jar' is a jar full of words of wisdom and encouragement, written by friends on pieces of paper, for mum to dip into when she feels in need of some kind and comforting words. Your friends and family can jot down little messages that let you know they have your back and want to offer you love, support and the knowledge that you can do this and that they are with you the whole way. Even the simplest words can make a huge difference when you're feeling overwhelmed. Perhaps they will say: 'You are an amazing mum', 'This too shall pass', 'Baby snuggles are the best, enjoy', 'Sleep is for wimps' or 'Know that you are loved'.

Mum friends

Another great source of support for a new mum, is fellow new mums. There is something so comforting about being with a group of women who are all going through the same things and being able to support each other. You may meet these mums through an antenatal class you have taken, local pregnancy or postnatal groups or breastfeeding cafés – you could even place an ad on your local community forum, asking if there are any new mums in your area that fancy meeting up for a cuppa.

Regular meet-ups with other mums create the opportunity to share advice, ask questions and offer support. Make sure, though, that you are with people who are equally as nurturing and be careful not to get caught in the dangerous trap of comparison and competition or 'one-up-mum-ship'. As all babies develop at their own pace, so do mothers. Remember we all have our own strengths and weaknesses and together we can help each other out. There is no such thing as the perfect mum, and if you manage to avoid 'competitive mum syndrome' you can create a wonderfully nurturing group that can become your tribe.

As the babies grow and you find your feet, you can then start to offer help and support and gifting time off to each other. Watch your friend's baby for a couple of hours one morning so that she can get on with stuff, and let her return the favour for you another day.

It's important to remember that by asking for help, you are at the same time giving people permission to reach out for help in return, and this is the basis of most long-lasting friendships.

You Are Still You

After you have a baby, it is very common to feel a little lost when it comes to your identity. In your life before becoming someone's mum, you may have studied hard and developed a career for yourself, travelled, enjoyed adventure with your partner and had a vibrant social life. Once a baby arrives (especially your first baby), amidst the birthing, feeding and caring for your little one around the clock, you may wonder where the old you has disappeared to.

Our mind needs significant support and encouragement as it adapts to this new normal with all its joys and challenges. During your pregnancy, you may have spent time thinking about the big changes that are coming your way. However much you consider it, though, it is very difficult to know how you will adapt to motherhood. We often imagine that our babies will fit into our lives, and not the other way around. However, these clever little humans have other plans and as new parents we learn quite quickly that, regardless of your baby's temperament, becoming a parent is likely to take a period of adjustment. Things that were important to us previously fall by the wayside and suddenly your full attention is taken up with the responsibility of another human's life, day and night. We have found that one of the issues that often arises with new mums is just how overwhelming adapting to being entirely responsible for another person can be.

We gain so much when our little one arrives, but we might find we miss certain parts of our old lives. Many women have told us that although they fell head over heels in love with their baby, they also grieved the life that they had very much enjoyed prior to having children, and that ache filled them with guilt. Honestly, it is absolutely okay – and totally normal! – to miss the get-up-and-go lifestyle that being child-free can bring. Getting a little pang for the part of yourself that enjoyed uninterrupted sleep, time to yourself, disposable income, carefree travelling or a challenging career is absolutely understandable. There is no need to feel guilty about missing that side of your life. Parenthood will bring you new adventures and enrich your life hugely but it just takes a while to adjust to such a big change.

It's also important to carve out some time for yourself to enjoy a little bit of the 'old you'. It is very restorative to occasionally release yourself from adult responsibility – you'll be filling your cup right back up to the top. (See also Freedom Friday on page 103.)

A FEEL-GOOD LIST

This is something we learned from a brilliant Australian midwife we worked with once. She told us that she gets her mothers to write a 'what makes me feel good' list. She explained that often when a family member offers to take the baby so that mum can have some downtime, she is so tired and out of the habit of doing stuff for herself that she actually can't think of anything nice to do. So write a list of all the things you know make you feel good – perhaps a bath, a nap, reading, painting your nails, a walk, anything that you know fills your cup and lifts your mood. Next time you are gifted some free time, you can just take a look and pick something off the list. No brain power needed!

Easy ways to retain your identity

- Plan a few much-needed nights out with your pre-baby friends and enjoy catching up on those important relationships that are outside of the motherhood bubble.

- Plan for your partner, friend, parent or whoever is able, to watch the baby for a little while so you can go for a run, take a Zumba class, go to a singing group or whatever it may be that acknowledges the pre-motherhood you!

- Read for pleasure. Not about which milestones your baby should be hitting and when, but about something that interests you outside of the remit of parenting. Perhaps you enjoyed comedy, travel, art or history before your attention became consumed with all things baby. Don't be afraid to revisit those subjects – it may just be the little bit of adult stimulation you were looking for.

- Write a feel-good list – see page 99.

- Get someone you trust to look after your baby and head out for a quick bite to eat with your partner somewhere not child-friendly. Try somewhere a little more grown-up and fancy than the local park café.

- Shake up your image a little. If your hair feels lank and shapeless, as does the faded array of maternity tops that you have been living in, make yourself an appointment to get your hair chopped or freshened up or treat yourself to a couple of new items for your wardrobe. You will be channelling your pre-motherhood inner style icon in no time.

'Just like that I was suddenly a mum. Nine months passed and I wasn't just Beth anymore. I was a mother too, and I think that's the proudest I had ever felt. But I still had to be me. I tried my best to balance my mum life with my old life and kept in touch with people as best I could. That whole support network was amazing and still is.'
~ Beth, mum of one

Alexis's freedom

friday

Let me tell you about how Freedom Friday was created. I remember it like it was yesterday. One evening when my son was nearly two and my daughter was five months old, I had come to the end of a pretty rough day in the land of motherhood. Bugs had hit our house, the kids had been cranky all day, I felt exhausted and when my son threw his dinner all over the floor I reached the end of my tether. At that point my phone rang and it was my husband saying he'd be home late from work. My heart just sank. Nonetheless I pulled myself together to get through bedtime. I bathed the kids, read them a story, popped them into bed and when my husband got home he found me sitting in the garden crying.

My energy levels were at an all-time low, my immune system was battered, I felt frumpy, fed up and my enthusiasm for motherhood had taken a bashing. I was trying to be all things to all people and I was failing to acknowledge that I needed a bit of time occasionally to fill my own cup up to the top, so I could continue to give my children the care and patience they deserved. In the end, my husband and I had a frank chat. He suggested to me that maybe a few hours away from our home during the week could help me to recharge. 'Freedom Friday' was coined.

For us, a Friday worked best as we knew that he could get home on time and I could head out to meet friends for a meal, drinks, catch a movie (sometimes on my own), go shopping or do whatever took my fancy. We started it that very next Friday. I went out for Mexican food with an old friend and drank red wine and we laughed until we cried. It was perfect. Knowing I could have that snippet of time to myself every week, to plan something that I had enjoyed before I became a mum just changed everything. I no longer felt fed up and stuck, sinking in the piles of laundry, functional cooking and kids' toys.

We appreciate it isn't always possible to actually go out, away from your home, in the early weeks and months. Feeding schedules and bedtimes can make it tricky. However, there are plenty of ways you can enjoy a mum's night off even in the comfort of your own home. Scheduling in an evening when you will let your partner, family member or friend take your little human for an hour or two while you have some well-deserved time out is so important.

Another way to carve out some time for yourself could be to do a 'freedom swap'. It may be that you have friends with babies a similar age to yours and they may well enjoy a couple of hours off duty just as much as you would. Talk to them and see whether they might like to look after your little one once a week or once a month while you get your hair cut or take an exercise class and then you can return the favour and help them out with a little bit of baby-free time.

It's so important to recognise early on that taking time out is not self-indulgent, it's essential. A happy mummy equals a happy baby. Taking that all-important time to refuel can often make you feel calmer and have more energy, which will not only benefit your little one in the long run but will also help you have the most enjoyable and fulfilling postnatal experience possible.

How would you spend your Freedom Friday?

Every time we run an antenatal class we ask our parents-to-be what they would do if they had a couple of child-free hours to themselves once a week. How would they fill their cup back up to the top? The most popular answers are:

AT HOME:

· Take a long sumptuous bath, lights low, candles burning.

· Listen to a relaxation track and calm that frazzled mummy brain.

· Read a book (so simple yet so hard when you have an unsettled baby).

· Take an online exercise class.

· Cook for pleasure, not for need.

· Relax in bed with your favourite music and drink.

· Do a face mask or paint your nails.

· Play a musical instrument.

OUT OF THE HOME:

· Have a meal and catch up with friends.

· Take a class and learn a skill.

· Catch a movie.

· Go to a gig.

· Go to the pub for drinks.

· Visit the hairdresser.

· Go for a run, swim, cycle, exercise class.

· Have a massage, facial, manicure or pedicure.

· Go shopping.

Although these activities may have seemed run of the mill before you had children, believe us, they become a real treat when your days and nights revolve around the needs of your little one. (See also 'The Importance of Rest, Part 1' on page 29 and 'The Importance of Rest, Part 2' on page 154.)

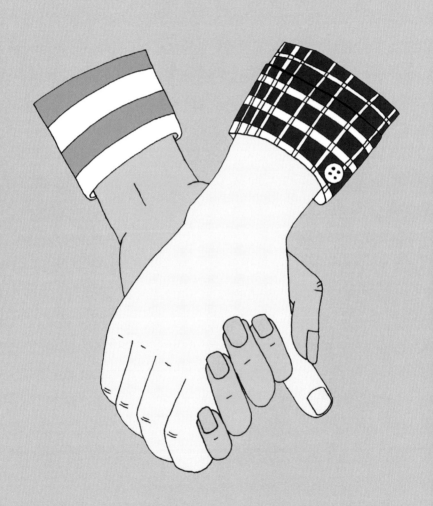

Self-care Tips For Your Relationship

We always encourage the couples we work with to think about how becoming parents may change their relationship.

Many say they expect it will bring them closer and this is certainly a plus side. Experiencing the journey of pregnancy and birth side by side and then looking after a brand-new tiny baby can really knit a relationship together. The early days are all about new parents adapting and supporting each other. Even our society recognises this, which is why your partner can take leave from work so you can adjust as a family unit in those first couple of weeks with a new baby.

However, as the weeks unfold, it is not unusual to feel more than a little stormy towards one another, to snipe when fatigue has set in and you are feeling depleted in energy and wildly emotional. After all, we tend to lash out emotionally at those we feel safest around and closest to. When you are both bone-tired and overwhelmed it is easy to take it out on each other, but this will likely pass before too long and there will come a point when you will be able to look back and in hindsight have a chuckle at the expense of the frazzled new-parent versions of yourselves.

Top tips for how not to hate your partner

1. Remember it's all new for them too and they are trying to get their heads around this colossal life change as much as you are. Yes, from the outside it may seem that their lives have stayed pretty similar to how they were pre-baby, but at the very least they are adjusting to more responsibility and less time with you all to themselves.

2. Do not bottle it up. There are likely to be times when they will say or do the wrong thing because they, like you, are only human. Consider how you are communicating with one another. For example, being passive aggressive is likely to push you further apart rather than bring you closer together. Talk to them and let them know what is helpful or what is making you feel frustrated. They are probably not psychic, so be open and honest about how you are feeling. And get them to open up about how they are feeling too.

3. Divvy up the chores. Save yourself the age-old argument of who is pulling their weight more around the house by being clear with each other about what needs to be achieved chore-wise. You are both likely to be busy and feeling short on time, so just team up and work out logistically how you can get it done.

4. Allow your partner time to bond with the baby. Remember that if your partner has returned to work, it is likely you are spending far more one-to-one time with your baby than they are, learning their subtle cues and establishing a loving and trusting relationship. Make sure your partner has some special time with their little one too. If they end up putting the nappy on back to front and

the baby grow on inside out, it's because they are still learning and just need some more practice. Don't laugh at their failed attempts but be grateful that they are trying and want to support you as much as possible. Point them in the right direction and help build their confidence as a new parent.

Don't fall into the resentment rut

Another issue that can arise as you adjust to motherhood and your new role of baby's main caregiver is resentment. Often women tell us that as their partners get up in the morning, casually get themselves ready for work and then skip out of the house, they feel a little bit annoyed that their life appears unburdened by responsibility. Often dialogues are opened between couples through cross words about whose life is now harder and who is feeling more exhausted. In those early days, it can feel like you are ships that pass in the night, only conversing about the amount and colour of your baby's poo or which one of you is more shattered. You know that you are on the same side, with the same goals, but tiredness and raw emotions can make you chip away at each other. Ultimately it is not a competition and digging yourself into a rut of resentment is not helpful for either of you. Talk calmly and openly, make plans together and see if you can pull in extra help and get some baby-free time as a couple. Remind yourselves why you came together in the first place.

Date night

We know it may seem completely obvious, but spending time as a couple after you have a baby is very important. Once you start to feel the fog of the first few months begin to lift, you might want to start carving out some time for each other.

It doesn't have to be anything big or fancy. See if you could get a friend or family member to watch your little one while you head out for a quick pizza or a drink. Catching a movie or going to a gig may be good respite but it won't give you the time to catch up with one another properly.

If your baby does not take any bottle feeds (expressed or formula) then keep it local! If you know that there is a window in between two breastfeeds, then plan your help to arrive so you have time to nip out for fish and chips around the corner, and then return home for the next feed. If your baby is unsettled then you can always be contacted and head home a little earlier.

Although it is easier said than done, you could even try to spend your hour or two together with a baby-chat ban! Your mind is still likely to be on your baby, but it can be refreshing to remind yourself that there were plenty of things to talk about before you became parents. You may find your mama heart wants to race back to your baby before too long, but even a little while completely focusing on your partner and enjoying one another's company can be hugely beneficial for the both of you.

Other easy ways to reconnect as a couple

- Have a bit of downtime on the sofa. Your baby may not be in a rhythm or routine yet so you may have them nearby, but snuggle up, get comfortable, lower the lights, play your favourite music, listen to a podcast or catch up on your favourite TV show. Alternatively, have a screen break: turn the box off, put your phones away and be completely present with one another.

- Give each other a massage. Check out our massage section on pages 53–58 for instructions for easy partner massages. Touch releases oxytocin, which is our love hormone, and massage can be a lovely and gentle reintroduction to being physical with one another again.

- Be in the same room. It is so easy to feel like ships that pass in the night when you have a little baby. If you or your partner are cooking, then join them in the same room if you are able to, even if that means one of you jiggles the baby while the other one cracks on with the meal.

- Remember to say 'thank you'. It is so easy in those early days to compare your transition to parenthood with one another's and accuse each other of getting off lightly. You may feel that your partner appears to be living the same life that they had pre-baby, while they may think you are enjoying extended annual leave, filled with tea, cake and mummy gossip. Neither of these notions are completely true. Life has changed for both of you, hugely. It is so important to remember you are part of the same team, your lives are interwoven and you are probably both working hard for the benefit of your brand-new family.

- Order a takeaway or cook up an easy meal and crack out the board games. We know this is not particularly rock and roll . . . but it can be a fun way of having a bit of 'couple time' at home.

- Send each other flirty texts. It can be good for the old self-esteem to let your partner know that you are thinking about them, even though you may be apart. There is nothing like a bit of flirty banter to add a spring to your step.

Calming the Mind When the Overwhelm Sets In

There will be days when our parenting will be on point, our baby will behave like a cherub and we will feel totally smug about how well we are nailing motherhood. There will also be days that follow sleepless nights, when we have no patience, a cranky baby and we find ourselves sobbing in unison with our little one. There is absolutely no shame in this and the majority of mothers will have days when they feel that it's all a little bit too much and they need to be held even more tightly and cocooned with an extra layer of TLC.

Top tips for those overwhelming days:

1. Know that you are not alone. You are not the first and you will certainly not be the last mother to feel overwhelmed.

2. Talk with friends who know you well, who you can be open and honest with and who can pump you up when you are a little out of your depth.

3. In brighter times, record the highs of motherhood – your positive experiences – in a journal or a notebook so that

you can access some spirit-lifting fist pumps when you are feeling like it's all a bit much. See below for more on this.

4. Try not to plan too much. Lowering your expectations of how much you should be achieving each day can make you feel more in control and as if you are actually achieving more. Think quality not quantity.

5. Remember that although the days may at times feel long, the months really do fly by and before you know it you will be celebrating your baby's first birthday and wondering where on earth the last year went.

Being a mother is a huge life change BUT you are enough, you are doing your best and sometimes motherhood is all things wonderful. However, there are also times when life just doesn't give us a break and we end up feeling out of control. Talking honestly with other mums about the many different shades of parenthood is good for everyone. You do not have to enjoy every second of the journey, but there will be many times that you will and you deserve to celebrate the great days.

When you have those wonderful moments that fill your heart up and lift your spirit, be sure to bank them. Perhaps fill a little notebook with short entries of all the lovely moments that bring you joy, such as precious skin-to-skin time with your baby, that incredible first smile, watching your partner bonding with the baby and perhaps even the supportive and kind new friends that have entered your life since becoming a mother. Then, if you have a day when you feel down, turn to those all-important happy memories and remind yourself how nothing is constant and you will have more of these good times ahead.

As you adjust to parenthood try not to plan too many activities. A jam-packed day can make you feel overwhelmed, chaotic and emotionally exhausted. Of course, it is important to get out now and then, move your body and get some fresh air or those walls will start to feel like they are closing in on you. However, remember your nights are still likely to be very broken so during the day try to conserve a little bit of your precious energy.

Ultimately, try to remember that the newborn months are short, with many passing phases and before you know it, it'll all seem like a distant memory. As you enter into each new stage, you will do so a little less tired and a whole lot more self-assured in the parent you are. You are in this for the long game, so it really doesn't matter if you had baked potatoes for dinner for the last four nights or that the washing pile is mounting. At this point all that really matters is that you nurture and support your postnatal mind and body, and care for your baby.

THIS TOO SHALL PASS

Ways to feel more in control:

- Pour yourself a cuppa and write a to-do list of everything that is making you feel discombobulated and then tick off the quick wins, such as texting your friend back with a date and time for them to pop over and meet your baby.

- Breathe. Close your eyes, relax your shoulders and take three deep breaths in through your nose out through your mouth. Also see our breathing exercises on pages 118–119.

- Breaking down the tasks that are necessary to keep a family home running can help you feel more in control. Be pro-active, prioritise the household jobs that are essential to helping you feel calm and split those tasks up between you and your partner.

- Get off social media for a bit if it is making you feel like everyone else is nailing this motherhood lark and you can't even seem to do the simplest task without the overwhelm setting in.

- Delegate. Hand some jobs over to your partner, friends, family and you will feel instantly lighter.

- Get a food delivery so you always have something nourishing to eat. Eating properly and regularly can really help you feel less anxious (see also page 60).

- Learn to say 'No'. We can feel totally overwhelmed if we end up doing too much. Learning to manage others' expectations of you is so important to make you feel more in control and under less pressure from the get-go.

'When you're having a day that just doesn't get going, your baby is crying and everything's a mess, then stuff some things in a bag (used to be nappy, dummy and bottle for me) and get out the house. It can feel impossible to leave sometimes but it's much better to cut your losses and go and sit in a café with a cup of tea having a cuddle with your baby. Feel the love not the stress! He or she will probably fall asleep by the time you're home and you can deal with the pigsty you left behind then. Everyone has bad days – even people that don't admit to them!'
~ Julia, mum of three

And breathe

Practising regular breathing techniques and mindfulness can really help to calm the mind when we're feeling overwhelmed. When everything gets on top of us, we release adrenaline, which can make us feel even more anxious and panicky. When the overwhelm sets in, becoming aware of our breathing can turn everything around and help us regain a sense of control.

Although there are many breathing techniques to choose from, we have included our two favourite exercises to help you release and reduce stress, anxiety and tension and help return you to a state of calm.

THE DOOR-FRAME BREATHING EXERCISE

- Make yourself comfortable.

- Find the doorway or obvious rectangle shape within the room where you are and focus on it.

- Relax your shoulders down and consciously let go of any tension your shoulders may be holding. Become aware of your breath.

- Breathe in through your nose as your eyes travel along the top of the doorframe (short side).

- On your outbreath purse your lips and blow that breath away, slowly, as your eyes travel down the long side of the doorframe. A longer out breath than in breath is very calming.

- Continue round the doorframe until any tension or overwhelm dissipates and you return to feeling calmer and more in control.

The ocean breath

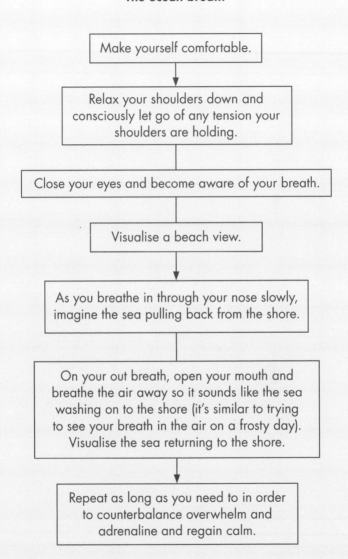

Make yourself comfortable.

Relax your shoulders down and consciously let go of any tension your shoulders are holding.

Close your eyes and become aware of your breath.

Visualise a beach view.

As you breathe in through your nose slowly, imagine the sea pulling back from the shore.

On your out breath, open your mouth and breathe the air away so it sounds like the sea washing on to the shore (it's similar to trying to see your breath in the air on a frosty day). Visualise the sea returning to the shore.

Repeat as long as you need to in order to counterbalance overwhelm and adrenaline and regain calm.

The new mum super-simple relaxation script

Lower the lights, sit comfortably and ask your partner to read these words to you, calmly and slowly. It is really important for them to pause in between each suggestion for at least ten seconds. You can also record yourself reading this script and then play it back to yourself.

I would like you to close your eyes, relax your shoulders down and become aware of your gentle, slow breath.

Notice how your chest rises and falls with each easy breath.

Become aware of any feelings of tension slipping away from you with every out breath, taking you to a deeply relaxed and comfortable place.

Notice how the material of your clothes feels against your skin.

And how the air feels against your cheeks, cool or warm.

Become aware of how your body is being supported by whatever you are sitting on.

Now take a moment to become aware of any sounds within the room.

Perhaps the sound of your own breath.

Or the sound of a clock ticking.

And now focus on the sounds from outside this room.

Perhaps birdsong . . . passing traffic . . . people walking . . . children playing.

(pause for 30 seconds)

Once again become aware of the sounds inside the room where you are now.

The air upon your skin.

The sensation of your body in contact with the surface beneath you.

Notice the relaxed position of your shoulders as they release any hidden tension.

And now focus on your calm and gentle breath once again.

Start to move your hands and feet a little.

And when you are ready, open your eyes, stretch and return to the room feeling relaxed and refreshed.

10 INSTANT MOOD LIFTS

1. BREATHE

Stop what you are doing and breathe, slowly and properly. Often when we are feeling anxious our breath becomes shallow, so we are not getting as much oxygen to the muscles and brain as we need – this can make us feel tired, sluggish and anxious. See pages 118-119 for our calm breath techniques.

2. DRINK MORE WATER

It may be that you have not even noticed that you are feeling the discomfort of dehydration. Pour yourself a lovely big glass of refreshing cold water, perhaps adding fresh fruit, mint or cucumber to jazz it up. Or, if you remember, fill up a jug the night before or at the start of the day with water and pop in mint, strawberries, sliced lemon or cucumber or whatever takes your fancy. Then you will have a ready-made drink on hand when you need it. Or try one of our smoothies on pages 66–67.

3. LAVENDER

Lavender is a natural sedative and can be calming when its scent is inhaled. Place one drop of lavender oil, plus one drop of carrier oil (such as grapeseed oil) in the palm of your hand. Rub your palms together, then cup your hands over your nose and mouth, close your eyes and inhale.

4. CRY IT OUT

A good cry helps your body release stress hormones and may flush out toxins. Research even suggests that our tears may contain different chemicals depending on the reason we are crying! Obviously, if you are crying a lot then this is not right! See page 127 for when it's okay to not be okay.

5. PHONE A FRIEND

Keeping in touch with your tribe can lift your mood immediately. Pick up the phone and call whoever makes you feel supported and nurtured. Having a laugh or a cry with someone who 'gets you' will remind you that you are absolutely not alone on your motherhood journey.

6. LIGHT

The environment you are in will have a direct effect

on how you are feeling.
If you are exhausted and
your day is feeling dark
and a little bleak, throw
open the curtains and let
in some uplifting daylight.
If you are feeling anxious
and overwhelmed, you may
benefit from turning the
lights down and making
your surroundings feel
cosy and calm.

7. MOVE

Whether it be a dance,
a stretch, a run up the
stairs or star jumps in the
garden (if your pelvic floor
is up to it!) get your body
jiggling and you will feel
the benefits very quickly.
See pages 46 and 171 for
more on exercise and
stretching.

8. MUSIC

Putting on your favourite
tunes can turn around the
way you are feeling in an
instant. If your mood is
a little flat why not bring
out the big tunes of your
youth. Those forgotten
songs of the nineties and
noughties will take you on
a fun little journey down
memory lane.

9. A CHANGE IS AS GOOD AS A REST

If the walls feel like they
are closing in around you
and you are starting to get
cabin fever, step outside
for some natural light and
fresh air. You don't have
to go far. It may just be
a wander into your garden,
or a brisk walk around the
block but changing your
surroundings can instantly
lift the funk you may have
found yourself in.

10. EARPLUGS

We're not saying shut off
and don't respond to baby;
on the contrary, a crying
baby often needs to be held
and jiggled and cuddled.
But the high pitch and
noise of their cry can be
very stressful and makes us
release cortisol — a stress
hormone which leaves us
feeling frazzled. Pop some
earplugs in, and you will
soften the noise of the cry
and feel instantly calmer,
while still dishing out the
much-needed mama hugs.

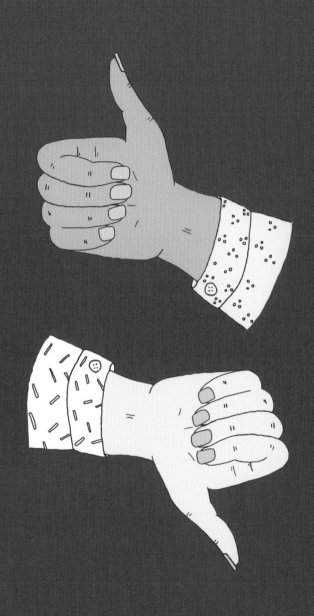

Debriefing the Birth

Having a baby is a pivotal life event. While some women find birth to be a positive and empowering experience, sometimes birth does not play out quite as we had hoped. We all know that there is no such thing as a textbook birth; each birth is unique and happens in its own way and at its own pace.

We have worked with many women over the years who felt that their emotional wellbeing was greatly affected by their birth story. Emotions are complex things, aren't they? Though you may wish you felt differently about how your birth played out, it is important to acknowledge that however you are feeling about your birth, what you are experiencing is true for you and you have no reason to feel guilty about those responses.

How birth is processed after the event is different for everyone, and there really is no right or wrong. If you still have questions about your birth as the days and weeks go on, you might find it helpful to open up an honest dialogue with your partner, midwife or doula quite early on about what you went through and how you are feeling. It's okay if it takes you a bit longer to seek out support though. If you're initially feeling too raw and find thinking about it triggers certain negative emotions, please don't feel you need to push yourself into addressing what happened until you're ready.

You might feel sad, angry, frustrated or shocked by what you have gone through and though you try, you may find it hard to explain these feelings as you process everything. Perhaps you have tried to tell friends and family about it but were met by well-wishers who don't know or can't understand how it feels for you, who underplayed your emotions and told you that, 'It's over now and at least you have a healthy baby to show for it? Right?'

However, it's not okay for you to have to shut your thoughts and emotions away and act like everything is fine. In fact, it is detrimental to your physical and mental wellbeing, as well as your relationship with your baby, partner, family and friends. You deserve to enjoy the experience of motherhood but sometimes the unpleasant thoughts and feelings surrounding the birth can block your joy from getting through. In the longer term, if left untreated and ignored, distressing experiences can spiral into birth trauma, which can lead to what is essentially post-traumatic stress disorder (PTSD) related to the birth of a baby. If this develops, a new mum may suffer with crippling anxiety, flashbacks, nightmares and guilt which can be terribly isolating. If you find yourself obsessing about the birth, suffering with anxiety and uncomfortable feelings, then reach out and discuss how you are feeling with your midwife, health visitor or GP. Most hospitals offer a debriefing service if you feel you need to speak to someone professional about your experience, usually after the initial six weeks have passed.

Whether you found your birth more difficult than you were expecting or more positive then you had imagined it might be, it can be helpful to write down your birth story and unpack how you are feeling about it. By doing this you can also open a conversion with your partner and remember the details together. If written down in a baby book or a journal, this can be lovely to share with your child when he or she is older.

Here are some questions to ask to get you started:

- How did labour start?
- Where were you when you had your first contraction?
- How did you feel?
- How long was your labour?
- Where did you give birth?
- How did you give birth?
- Who was there?
- What did you say when you first met your baby?
- How did your partner feel when they first held the baby?
- How long did you stay in hospital? (If you were in hospital at all.)
- What did it feel like when you came home from the hospital, or when your midwives left after a home birth?

If you're not okay, say something

After the baby is born a new mum often feels ALL the emotions! You can feel on cloud nine initially and pumped with the love-inducing oxytocin, only to come down with an exhausted bump a few days later as tiredness sets in and your hormones try to rebalance themselves. So much is changing for a woman during pregnancy, birth and the postnatal period that it is hardly surprising that she may feel her mental health is affected. Feeling a little anxious about how birth will play out, considering your baby's wellbeing once it's born and preempting how life as you know it may change will all get you thinking (sometimes a little too much).

Sometimes becoming a mother can stir up emotions from our childhood and about our relationship with our parents. Often this settles as we adjust from being a daughter to being a mother in our very own little family. If the feelings do not settle of their own accord, though, it can be useful to access some talking therapies to help you process these emotions. Speak to your GP, health visitor or midwife for help with this.

Baby blues

No matter how you birthed your babe you are likely to have moments where you feel rather fragile as your body begins the healing process and your birthing hormones settle. On top of this you have a tiny human who needs your care around the clock. Tiredness can play a huge role in making you feel overwhelmed – there is a reason sleep deprivation is used as a form of torture! After the first couple of days with a new baby it is very common for new mums to experience a bit of a slump and feel quite low. Mums often mention to us that they are feeling very emotional but don't exactly know why. This is likely to be the baby blues and affects about 80 per cent of women to some extent.

Symptoms of the baby blues can include:

- Irritability.
- Exhaustion.
- Tears that can be euphoric or terribly sad, but you're not able to pinpoint why.
- Mood swings.
- Overwhelmed by everything.
- A lack of concentration.
- Changes in appetite and ability to rest.

As with every issue to do with your mood, there is absolutely NO shame in feeling that way and talking about it with your partner, a friend, midwife, health visitor or GP can help a lot, even if it's just to get a bit of reassurance.

The baby blues will usually pass within a few days and by the second week after your baby's arrival, you should feel a little bit more in control once again.

In the meantime, try the following ways to give you a little pick-me-up to reassure you that you will be okay:

- Dim the lights and listen to some mindfulness, relaxation or positive affirmation tracks.

- Create a playlist of music that anchors you into a calm state.

- Lavender bath: add 6 drops of relaxing lavender essential oil to 1 tablespoon of full-fat milk (or grapeseed oil) and stir into a warm bath. (The milk or oil stops the essential oil from sitting in globules on top of the water.)

- Keep visitors to a minimum so you have time to rest (see page 77).

- Book in for a postnatal massage so you feel nurtured.

- Ditch the caffeine, as this can make you feel even more emotional and on edge.

- Practise restorative breathing techniques (see pages 118–119).

- Allow your partner, family and friends to help when they can (see page 79).

- Try using essential oils: tangerine, grapefruit, bergamot, geranium, rose, lavender and sweet orange are fantastic oils for the postnatal period. Avoid putting the oils on your skin, so that baby's delicate skin doesn't come into direct contact with them, but diffuse them in an oil burner to fill your room with their gorgeous fragrance, or dot them on a tissue to sniff at your leisure.

- Try to fulfill your basic needs of good hydration and nutritious food (see page 60–75).

- Doodle or colour in. Although adult colouring may seem a little faddy, it's popular for a reason as it can really help focus concentration and calm an anxious mind.

- Distract yourself with feel-good films, book and music. Steer clear of anything too heavy, dark or harrowing as it may make you feel more anxious and tense. Now's the time for some comedy!

- Gentle movement. Getting your body moving will help you to release wonderful feel-good endorphins. You are still very early on in your postnatal journey, though, so go slow – refer to our postnatal stretches on pages 46–52 and yoga sequence on pages 174–177 to help you move the right way and at the right pace.

- Keep a gratitude diary and try to think of a few things every day that are making you happy, even if it's as simple as a hot shower, or a walk in the park with your baby in the sunshine.

Postnatal depression (PND) and postnatal anxiety

Sometimes in the midst of the exhausting and overwhelming postnatal fog, we don't seem to notice that at some point we really have stopped feeling okay and that our mood is no longer just down to tiredness. As women, we are so good at just getting on with it, being careful not to make a fuss and busying ourselves with the needs of others that we neglect to take note of whether we are actually feeling well ourselves.

Postnatal depression and/or anxiety affects approximately one in ten women. The figures are likely to be a lot higher than this as many women never reach out, so it is really hard to get exact statistics. But the bottom line is, it is very common. It can usually start from around three weeks after baby has been born and can either stem from pre-existing conditions or swoop in for the first time in your life, out of the blue.

The human brain is beyond complex and, honestly, we don't know exactly why postnatal depression and anxiety (and other conditions) affect some women and not others. Every woman's brain will go through changes during pregnancy that make them feel a little fuzzy. This is sometimes referred to as having 'baby brain' and is likely to be a very clever way to make us less focused on the complicated issues of life and more dedicated to meeting the basic human needs of our little ones.

Sometimes the human brain gets into a bit of a muddle. Perinatal mental health conditions are often linked to chemical or hormonal imbalances in the brain. There is research to suggest that during the pregnancy and postnatal period, some women are extremely sensitive to reproductive hormones and this directly affects their mental health. This can develop into conditions affecting their mood, such as anxiety, depression and obsessive compulsive disorders.

Women who experience worrying thoughts and feelings might not want to talk openly about it for fear of judgement. But consider this: you wouldn't walk around on a broken leg and pretend that everything was okay, so why should you have to carry on with a debilitating condition that effects your mental health?

However postnatal depression manifests, it is likely to make a new mum feel very unhappy and worried. Don't suffer in silence, afraid to utter the words to your partner or a health professional for fear of what they will think. By opening up and sharing your thoughts and feelings you may actually disempower the terrible depression and anxiety by 'calling it out' so to speak. Most importantly you will be opening the door to the support and treatment that you may need. It is not enough to just be surviving. You have the right to experience the joys that motherhood brings, so reach out and take the first step to recovering. See page 191 for further resources on mental health.

Alexis's experience of perinatal depression

I know first-hand what this debilitating condition can feel like and as a midwife I am passionate about talking openly about my own experience. For me, it began at around twenty-two weeks of pregnancy. I started to find myself worrying a lot and about quite irrational things.

Now I should tell you I have suffered in recent years from low-level anxiety and have had some amazing therapy for it. I had lost my wonderful dad to cancer six years prior to this pregnancy and noticed I was thinking about him at the end of his life more often. That in itself is not odd; many people tell me that they think more about death when they become parents. There is something about our fragile existence and our innate desire to protect our babies from harm that seems to have us thinking more about the unthinkable.

It started with a really bizarre and strange thought. I was putting up some pictures in my house and as I banged the nail into the wall I had a frightening and strange thought about someone breaking into my house and attacking me and my children with a hammer. Normally someone would just think, 'what a strange thought', put it to the back of their mind and forget about it. I couldn't. I freaked out. My anxiety rocketed and I found myself checking all the windows and doors obsessively and truly starting to believe that it was going to happen. The harder I tried not to think about it, the more it consumed my mind. After a few days the thought started to fade, but another one grew in its place, again based around harm coming to my family.

I felt completely on my own. I was hardly sleeping, it felt uncomfortable just to be in my own skin. I flitted between agonising fear and vacant emptiness. If anyone mentioned my growing bump or pregnancy to me I wanted to burst into tears. Now as you know I am a midwife, so how did I not know what was happening to me? But I kept thinking: What if this was my life now and I would never get back to the happy and enthusiastic me that I'd always been?

I finally reached out to an amazing friend who had experienced the most hideous and debilitating postnatal depression. I slowly and cautiously started to tell her how I was feeling and how tortuous my life had become. She was incredibly kind and we started messaging each other every day. I would send her long rambling messages about the overwhelming thoughts and all the feelings, oh the feelings! I found this so helpful but through speaking to her I realised I needed professional help so that I could climb out of this pit.

I was encouraged to join an anxiety and depression CBT (cognitive behavioural therapy) course to learn to control my thoughts and behaviours. I was so worried about sharing such intimate details with strangers but it ended up being one of the most liberating things I have ever done. Everyone there had their own personal experiences of anxiety and depression and I ended up getting to know some of the kindest, most genuine folk I have ever met. I was no longer alone in my suffering and I started to truly believe I was going to get better.

As the weeks continued I began to start living again and enjoying my life. Labour started on my due date and I had the most empowering and calm birth. In the following days I had extra support at home from visiting midwives as you are more likely to experience PND if you have suffered with a mental health problem during pregnancy. I was lucky though and felt very well both mentally and physically.

Since I started talking about my experience with perinatal anxiety and depression, it has amazed me how many people have said, 'Me too!'. We must continue to speak out! If you are feeling like you are facing this on your own, please know that there is help out there. You are not alone.

'In the midst of severe postnatal depression, I was encouraged to take my baby swimming. As I got into the pool, I had to hand him over to the instructor and my heart pulled. For the first time I actually felt something and I knew this was a turning point and I would get better. I was keeping a mood diary and that was the first positive entry!'
~ Mary, mum of one

you're doing an
ama
job

zing

Motherhood will teach you more about yourself than you can ever imagine. Yes, there will be times when things don't go to plan and you feel that overwhelm creep in, but it won't last. You will gently adjust to this new role as the weeks and months pass by and some days you will fly high and others you will fly by the seat of your pants. That's motherhood, but that's also life full stop!

Try not to focus on the things that are not going right, that are out of your control or are making you feel that you are not the perfect mum. The notion of perfection simply does not exist and can be really damaging to your happiness. Instead, when things don't go quite right, try to keep calm and relaxed. Tomorrow really is another day and another chance to parent to the best of your ability. There is no way you can be completely in control and nail it all the time, and by acknowledging that and being kind to your mental wellbeing as well as your physical healing, you are likely to feel much more confident and fulfilled on your motherhood journey.

guiding

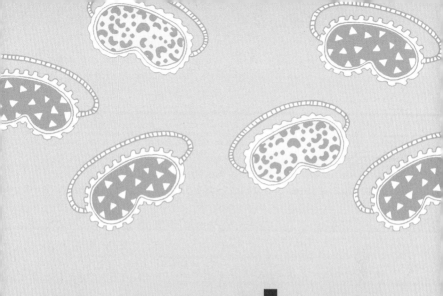

a mother

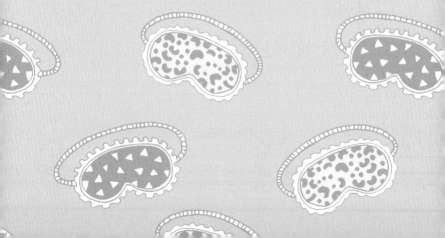

Alongside your physical and mental wellbeing, we also want to support and guide you as the postnatal weeks unfold and you gently ease yourself back into some of the activities and exercises you enjoyed pre-baby. When and how to go about getting a bit of that normality back into your life post-baby is something that comes up a lot when we speak to the mums we care for. At some stage, you will also feel like regaining some intimacy with your partner and when and how is the right time for this is also a question we are often asked.

In this part of the book, our aim is to guide you by supplying you with as much information, supportive advice and simple tips as we can to help you on your way back to enjoying ALL of the different elements of your life. But remember, we only hope to provide you with advice and information – respecting and trusting yourself as you navigate your way through motherhood is so important. We all have individual preferences when it comes to parenting style, in part dictated by the fact that not all babies are the same! Perfect parenting doesn't exist, so stop aiming for it. Remember that your way really is OK. Open the doors to trusting your instinct and intuition, let go of comparisons and enjoy the style and rhythm of your own motherhood journey.

After your baby is born, attention very quickly shifts to taking care of them and their needs. There are so many books written on this subject: how to parent, how not to parent, different types of parents, and how each type of parenting affects the child. And it's not just books, there are blogs and vlogs and websites and TV programmes too. While it is amazing to have so much information at our fingertips, it can also be incredibly overwhelming and sometimes makes us lose confidence in our mothering instincts.

If this is your first baby, you may have no idea what kind of parent you want to be and that is absolutely fine! Until you are holding that baby in your arms and dealing with the day-to-day logistics of feeding, bathing, clothing and sleeping – not to mention the hundreds of nappy changes – it's all a bit abstract and can be hard to get your head around. Alternatively, some of us enter into parenthood with lots of ideas and ideals about what we will and won't do as parents. If this is you, remember that it isn't black and white – it's a very big mass of grey.

We want you to enjoy motherhood and not be overcome with self-doubt. Be kind to yourself as you find your way, and don't give yourself a tough time. Be flexible where possible and gentle with yourself when things don't go to plan. We have had clients who were absolutely adamant they were going to keep their baby close to them in a sling constantly, but discovered they couldn't because they found it a bit claustrophobic. Other parents thought they were going to be very strict with their routine, but found they needed a more flexible approach for their own wellbeing. You won't know what works for you until you give it a go, so just remember to give yourself space to find your way.

You will undoubtedly be offered many opinions from all corners! Some will be incredibly helpful, while others will not. Often you won't be able to put into words why it might not feel right, so follow your gut and trust your instinct. Although advice almost always comes from a place of love, often others will be projecting their own experience on to you, and this isn't their story, it's yours, so do what feels right for you. Learn to take advice that feels helpful, while politely ignoring that which doesn't. Remember that your way is OK! In fact, it's better than OK, it's perfect! There is no 'one size fits all' and your baby is developing their very own pattern and personality; after all, they are a real living human, not a Tamagotchi.

A Mother's Instinct

A mother's instinct is no joke. In fact, we have many midwives and doctor friends who talk about how seriously they take a mother's intuition in their work and there have been many studies around this subject. You may find you wake up just before your baby wakes up for a feed, or you check on baby just as they are waking up. All of these things happen because somehow we are so wonderfully tuned in to our babies and can react accordingly. At the end of the day, out of all the people around you, if for no other reason than just the sheer amount of time you spend with your baby, you WILL absolutely know them better than anybody else.

It is easy to accidently disempower a new mum, so we must be very careful with the language we use around them. We see this often with a throwaway comment made by a well-meaning relative, such as 'Oh, he's playing you, just put him to sleep in his cot otherwise you'll be making a rod for your own back.' Sadly this can lead to a new mum, who wants nothing more than a snuggle with her baby but fears making this so-called rod, putting her baby into its cot, denying herself some amazing early bonding.

We remember working with a new mum once who had had a very quick and gentle birth and who was so happy and calm with her new baby. She seemed to be very intuitive, not at all fearful and not once doubting her ability, and looked as though she'd had many children before. She decided to go for a little walk along the ward with her baby, and was quickly told off very sternly by a midwife, who told her that she should absolutely not be walking around with a baby in her arms in case she dropped him, and she must instead push him around in a cot. The mum's persona changed immediately and she became very worried and anxious and kept second-guessing herself. It was a clear example of accidental disempowerment of that new mum. The midwife didn't mean to upset her, she was just following hospital policy which, for health and safety reasons and the risk of legal action, tried to ensure that no babies were accidently dropped. But for a delicate new mum, this interaction made her completely distrust her instinct and for a good few hours after that, she asked permission to pick her baby up.

Doubt can also come from within ourselves. We see this sometimes after a woman has experienced a birth that perhaps didn't go quite as she had wanted, and she is left feeling disappointed or let down by her own body and not quite trusting herself. A birth not going to plan, however, does not mean your body does not know how to care for the baby you have birthed or that you can't do it! Give your body and yourself a chance and let them do you proud.

It is Not a Competition

- This is not a competition and therefore you cannot lose; you and your baby will find your own way of doing things at a pace that is right for you. Forget the one-up-mum-ship! This is not a race, it is a journey that you are on with YOUR own baby.

- Consider the long run. You are a mother now and sometimes you are going to feel like you are a bit late to the party and sometimes you will feel like you and your child are ahead of the game. The same applies to other mums you come into contact with and that is OK, motherhood is ongoing. You can learn from each other.

- Be kind to yourself, you are doing the best that you can at the moment, and so are the other mums around you.

- Try to celebrate the milestones of other mums and their infants, and you will find that they will often be delighted to hear about the achievements of your motherhood journey too!

- Remember that we tend to reveal the best bits. Bear in mind that all you know about other people's lives is what they share with you. It may or may not be completely accurate. Other mums may not be sharing the tough times, but rather showing us a snapshot of life through rose-tinted specs. Remember that this is often the case with social media.

ESCAPING THE FAILURE TRAP

You may not be having the best day — perhaps everyone else is acting like mothering is a piece of cake or their baby is just so chilled out and easy-going and it gets you wondering, what am I doing wrong? If you're feeling that little voice inside, making you feel like a failure and you need reminding just how important and worthwhile you are, then this little list is for you.

- You are the mum to your baby. In the end, it doesn't really matter what other babies are achieving or how other mums are parenting their infants. You are the expert of your own baby and most likely able to meet their needs by following your own intuition.

- Consider all the little things that you have achieved since your baby has arrived: navigating each hour of each day with this tiny human, feeding them, changing them and meeting their needs while healing yourself and adjusting to parenthood. You are awesome so try not to be so hard on yourself.

- Focus on the good bits. We can guarantee that if you hear ten good things and one bad thing about your baby and your parenting, the message you will take away with you will be the negative one. Other mums, family members and even partners will have ideas about how best to bring up baby. Take away the bits that are useful and disregard what does not work for you. You cannot please everyone.

- Know that your baby only has eyes for you. Seriously, they learn pretty fast that with mum comes comfort, warmth and security. No matter how tough you're finding today, how messy your house is or how out of tune you sound as you try desperately to settle your baby with a made-up lullaby, your baby thinks you are the bee's knees.

What if You Don't Bond With Your Baby Straight Away?

Sometimes if a mum has had a difficult labour, or perhaps her hormones are unbalanced, she may not experience that rush of oxytocin we often talk about after birth. Please do not worry if you feel that you are not immediately bonding with your baby; there are many reasons women may not feel this immediate rush of the love hormone. Often with a little talking, rest and reassurance, mum is able to experience the feelings of bonding with her baby soon enough. If the feelings of disconnect continue, please do speak to your midwife, health visitor or GP who will be able to help you access some extra support and care.

Here are some of our top ways to encourage oxytocin and baby bonding.

- **Talk:** Let people know how you are feeling. There is nothing wrong with needing a little time to connect with your baby. It doesn't mean you are a bad parent and it doesn't mean you won't connect; you just need to give it time.

- **Skin-to-skin contact:** It's okay if you don't feel like doing this straight away, but in the days and weeks, even months, following birth, try to have as much skin-to-skin with your baby as you can. This is the quickest way to release oxytocin, our lovely bonding hormone. Use this time to take rest and learn about your little one. Sometimes it's just a matter of getting to know this little character who has just entered our lives.

- **Sniff your baby:** Babies smell delicious. Smelling your baby's head as you snuggle them or wear them in a sling can give you a rush of the love hormone.

- **Bathe with your baby:** A great way of having skin-to-skin; your baby will love the feel of the water on their body in the safety of their mama's arms.

- **Dance:** We know this may be the last thing you feel like doing, but dancing with your baby can be a great way to release endorphins, our feel-good hormones, and make you feel more connected to your baby. Turn up the radio and have a little boogie. As they get older you will notice how much they enjoy having a jiggle with you too. There are even mum and baby dance classes around if you need a little help.

Interpreting Baby Cues and Communication

A common concern we hear a lot from new mums is: 'Everybody else but me seems to know the different cries for hunger and tiredness, how the hell do you tell the difference?' Although it is impossible to be 100 per cent sure what a baby is trying to say to you through their cries, noises and actions, we can often play detective and try to work out whether they are in need of something or whether they are just entertaining themselves. Remember it is a bit of a guessing game and it takes time and patience on both sides. This is much easier without the noise of the outside world distracting you both and it is one of the reasons we are big advocates of slowing it down and really taking time to quietly be with your newborn in those early weeks.

Sometimes, we never fully get it – some cries are harder to read than others and sometimes even baby isn't quite sure what it is they need at that moment; they just know they're not feeling right. We are not mind readers, so don't give yourself a hard time if you can't translate the meaning of every different pitch of cry!

Your baby will probably not display all of the cues below so just take note of the indicators that are relevant for you and them.

Hunger cues
- Rooting (opening their mouth and pecking around to find the food).
- Sucking on their fist, your finger, your chin or anything they can get to.

- Licking or smacking their lips or sucking on their tongue.
- Crying – but this will often come later than the other cues listed above.

Stimulation/play cues
- Physically alert.
- Smiling – if they have started doing this (usually after six weeks).
- Gazing at you or at an object of interest.
- Mirroring you by poking out their tongue or blinking both eyes.
- Taking your finger and grasping it tightly.

Tired cues
- Becoming quiet, less active or turning away from you (disengaging).
- Yawning.
- Frowning.
- Fussing or crying.
- Trying to rub eyes or ears (comes later as newborn babies are not able to control their hands well enough to do this).
- Not engaging with feeding.

Pain/discomfort/unwell cues
- Intense, high-pitched or longer-lasting cries.
- Rigid, tense or scrunched up in the body (often if they have trapped wind and have sharp pain in their tummy) or perhaps too limp.
- Grimacing, frowning, looking away from you.
- Their sleep rhythm changes (if they have a pattern to their sleep/waking cycle).

'Parenting was so much easier when
I raised my non-existent children
hypothetically: don't be afraid to rip up
your rule book when baby is here. So you
never wanted to co-sleep but now he only
wants to sleep in your arms? If it feels like
the right thing to do, then go for it. Baby
was going to have a strict schedule and
only sleep in her cot? And now she only
naps long enough when she's in the buggy?
Get out there and enjoy a new routine.
Whatever works for you and your baby
is more important than any self-imposed
judgement you laid out beforehand. You are
not a failure because you are not meeting
the standards of pre-parent you. You are
a glorious success negotiating your way
through the needs of a tiny human being,
and every day you are learning a little
bit more.'
~ Nicola, mum of four

Your Baby Needs Time Too

Your little one is adjusting to life on the other side too! The twelve weeks following birth are now known as 'The Fourth Trimester', and it makes perfect sense that your baby needs time to settle into their new world just as much as you do. When responding to your little one's needs, consider how much they have to adapt once they are born.

WOMB DWELLING

- Warm (at body temperature).
- Dark (with a pinky hue).
- No awareness of gravity.
- Muffled sound due to amniotic fluid.
- Sounds and vibrations of heartbeat, breathing, umbilical cord pulsing, digestion.
- Surrounded by water.
- No hunger.
- No tiredness.
- Constant rocking and moving.
- Contained and cosy.
- Has never had their skin touched by another human.

WORLD DWELLING

- Aware of feeling hot/cold.
- Different levels of brightness and darkness.
- Loud sounds.
- Dry.
- Aware of hunger.
- Aware of tiredness.
- Often still.
- Uncontained and able to stretch out.
- Touched and held by others.

The changes that a baby goes through are huge. Some babies seem to make the transition smoothly and appear to be calm and settled from early on, but don't be alarmed if your baby seems more sensitive to the change in their environment. They are little bundles of senses and we need to give them time and to gently support them as they adjust.

If you have had a long, rough night with your little one, we ask that you refer back to the lists above and think about all the changes that they are adapting to. Every time someone says, 'I wouldn't rock them to sleep if I was you, you will end up doing it every night,' consider the fact that your baby has never experienced complete stillness before and they might find it uncomfortable.

If you sense they may be feeding for comfort rather than hunger, contemplate the notion that in that moment they are feeling calm because of the sensation of being held and relaxed as they pacify themselves with their sucking reflex. If you find that they scream like a banshee every time you undress them for a nappy change or a bath, remember that they are getting used to the sensation of cooler air on their skin.

Enjoy helping them navigate this strange new world and revel in the fact that you are getting to know their little personality as they grow and develop day by day. They will get there, but we need to be kind to ourselves and stop doubting our natural response to the needs of our little one and acknowledge that it will take a little while for them to get used to their new home, out here in the big wide world.

The Importance of Rest, Part 2

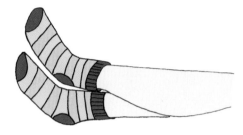

With a new baby the nights of broken sleep can sometimes feel like they will never end. Although every child is different, at some stage most children will settle into a pattern of sleep at night and this will give you the chance to recoup from those early days and weeks. When you are in the thick of sleepless nights and overwhelmed by 'bed dread', try to remember that the early stage of motherhood, which is when you tend to experience the most extreme broken sleep, WILL pass eventually. It won't be for ever. In the meantime, though, be patient with your little one and try to accept this as your new normal for a while, rather than wishing time away. Understanding how your baby might be feeling too can help you feel less frustrated (see page 152) and read our tips for how to maximise your sleep and rest time (on the following pages and see also pages 29–31).

It is normal and essential for newborns to feed around the clock so that they can grow and develop properly. However, it can be quite a shock for you adjusting to this new routine, where your sleep pattern is entirely determined by another human's schedule. We cannot put a specific time frame on how long it will take for babies to fall into a regular pattern and 'sleep through the night'. There are times when we just have to be realistic and patient with our little ones, understand that this is normal infant behaviour and just like every other part of their lives, they are learning how to do it, at their own pace.

Like anything else in life, this stage will move on to the next, and you may find you actually miss those quiet times together during the early months when your baby was tiny, when the world was sleeping and you were gently getting to know each other.

When you feel like you haven't slept for a hundred years

- **Sleep when baby sleeps!** Yes, we appreciate this is sometimes easier said than done, especially when it seems like the only time you can get chores done, or you have a toddler in tow, but whenever possible, make it happen.

- **Snuggle down with the older siblings as baby naps.** It may be that you have an older child that is no longer napping. If so, allocate baby's nap time to having quiet time together. Get the cosy blankets out, snuggle up on the sofa, watch an episode of their favourite children's programme or listen to music and just relax.

- **Allocate chore times.** If there are certain jobs around the home that you know will agitate you if left undone, designate specific times to do them. Try and split them up with your partner where possible. For example, they take the baby when they get home so you can sort out some laundry and then you take the baby for a feed while they make dinner.

- **Tag-team sleeping in the evening or on the weekend.** We appreciate you may not be able to do this all the time but scheduling in times when you tag team the parental duties can really help when you are bone-tired. For example, arrange that you will feed the baby at 8 or 9pm then hand the baby straight to your partner to settle while you go and get ready for bed, snuggle down and get straight to sleep if possible. Meanwhile, your partner will stay up to feed and settle baby the next time they wake with either expressed breast milk or formula depending on how you are feeding them. Then the next feed, you can take over and they can get some rest, and so on.

- **Get the family over.** Get a member of family or close friend to come over and take baby while you get some rest. Again, you could pre-arrange a bottle of expressed breast milk, or show them how to make up a bottle of formula milk and then head to bed and get some much-needed shut-eye.

WHAT IF MY BABY DOESN'T TAKE MILK FROM A BOTTLE?

This can feel extremely stressful, and as if it's impossible to catch a break. Rest assured, you CAN still take some time out. Follow all our top tips on taking a break, but discuss with whoever is looking after baby for you that they will need to bring baby to you for a feed, and then take them away again afterwards to allow you to continue to rest.

Evening lie-in

One of the things that often comes up about
sleep is that apart from solid uninterrupted
sleep, mums also miss a good old restorative lie-in.
In the early days, you may find yourself in bed in the
mornings with your baby as they often settle for a couple
of hours, especially after they have kept you on your toes
during the night. However, it's not quite the same as enjoying
a lazy morning sipping tea and reading a book in bed at
your leisure, with no one else's agenda to consider.

For the time being, while your baby is young, you are
going to have to change the way you plan your lazy lie-ins.
One way we like to suggest new mums can get more time to
themselves resting, is to have an evening lie-in. In order to
make the most of this and enable you to fill your cup back up,
set aside an evening that will work for you and your partner
and arrange the following:

- Plan your lie-in for an evening when your partner or
  close friend is available to take your baby. Prepare any
  expressed milk or formula that may be required in order
  to give yourself some uninterrupted time. If your baby
  doesn't use a bottle, start your lie-in just after a feed,
  so that you get the maximum amount of time to yourself
  after. If baby needs more milk, they can be brought to
  you for a feed, and then taken away again so that you
  can continue to rest.

- DO NOT be tempted to get caught up in finishing a few
  chores that are still on the to-do list.

- Run yourself a lovely relaxing lavender bath. Add 6 drops
  of lavender essential oil to 1 tablespoon of full-fat milk (or

grapeseed oil). Then stir this into the bath. (This will help the calming oil blend into the water and not sit on the top as little globules.)

- Turn the lights down low, light a candle and relax.

- Once out of the bath, get into your cosiest PJs and hop straight into bed.

- Try to leave your phone outside your room so you are not tempted to tap into the world outside your front door.

- Once in bed, sip tea, read a book, flick through a magazine, put on a mindfulness track, listen to your favourite music or doze.

- Take this time to put yourself first and refuel.

A couples lie-in

One of the main things many new parents tell us they miss is spending time together as a couple. Sometimes it's just the little things like lazy weekend mornings lounging around in bed. If you have a family member or friend staying who is able to look after baby for you for a bit, why not have an evening or afternoon lie-in with your partner! Follow the steps above, but snuggle up together. You may be so tired all you want to do is sleep, but snuggle up and sleep together, and you'll enjoy the closeness this brings. If you can't get someone else to watch your baby for you, keep baby in the room but still snuggle down with your partner and spend the afternoon there together – even if you're doing nothing. It's more about carving out the time to be together rather than what you are actually doing.

'I remember feeding Edith in the dead of the night, the witching hour when everyone else was fast asleep and it felt like I was the only exhausted still-awake person in the world. I had an overwhelming sense that this would never end. I wanted to scream and push her away from me, but hold her close and just will her to sleep all at the same time. I want to tell you that it does pass. It's not quickly, but it's too quickly. It stretches a thousand life times and is over in the blink of an eye. Try, please try, to rest when you can. Life with a baby who is constantly breastfeeding is so hard and you need to allow yourself to accept that.'
~ Harriet, mum of three

Feeding Your Baby

Babies feed so frequently because they have only tiny stomachs when they are first born, roughly the size of a small marble. It is very normal for a new baby to be asking for food every two to three hours at first. As the days pass, that little tummy of theirs will expand and their digestive system will jump into action. By day ten, their stomach will be roughly the size of a ping pong ball, and as they mature and take bigger feeds, you will start to get more of a break in between meal times.

Try and keep your days simple in the early postnatal period, and remember your biggest focus right now is on feeding and comforting your baby. If we face these early weeks knowing that these will be our main tasks, we won't feel quite so frustrated when we find ourselves with our babe in arms feeding constantly. It is interesting that in cultures where women take a longer rest after birth, and are left alone with baby to establish feeding – breast or bottle – they seem to enjoy and embrace this period more. Keep it simple to start, and remember, they grow up fast. Soon enough you'll be wondering where those baby days went, so try and enjoy them as much as you can now.

Breastfeeding

Once baby is born, your breasts are primed and ready for feeding to commence. However, don't be surprised if you need lots of support at first (even if it is not your first child). Your little one also needs time to learn this new skill and it's not at all unusual for it to take up to six weeks to settle into a rhythm that works for you both. Every time they feed, your breast and your brain communicate and the next order of milk is placed, which is why we always suggest you follow your baby's lead when it comes to feeding times (unless they are taking some convincing, then we need to lead them).

Our top ten tips for good attachment and breastfeeding:

1. Early on, encourage lots of skin-to-skin with access to your breasts. This does not have to be with you actively encouraging them on to the breast but can start with baby lying on you in the middle of your chest. Put baby there while they are calm and alert and let them explore and look for the areola and nipple. While they lick, touch and smell your breast area it will encourage that lovely oxytocin to flow which will help release your milk.

2. Look out for subtle hunger cues. When your baby is screaming its head off, it's usually passed the initial hunger stage. Early cues include licking their lips or poking out their tongue, salivating, bobbing their

head, opening their mouth and shaking their head, sucking fingers/thumb/fist, etc. If possible, avoid dummies at this time as you may miss feeding cues. Saying this, some babes are super sucky and even after lots of feeding, want to suckle for comfort. If mum (or her boobs) need a break, then using a dummy (while keeping an eye out for hunger cues) can be helpful. (See pages 149–150 for more on baby's cues.)

3. Position your baby well: tummy towards your tummy and nose to your nipple. Make sure their ears, shoulders and hips are aligned, as it's hard for them to eat while craning their neck. And always bring the baby to your breast! No one enjoys a game of bungee nip.

4. Open their mouth wide then help bring them on to the whole breast. They need to take in the areola, not just the nipple. As they create a seal with their mouth you want to see very little of the areola. If you see any at all it should be above their top lip and not below their bottom lip (think moustache, not beard).

5. If it hurts or continues to be uncomfortable then pop your little finger into the corner of their mouth to break the seal, get them off the boob and reposition. If the nipple looks pinched or misshapen afterwards then the attachment was not quite right. It should look exactly the same shape after a feed as before, as it should be gently pressing on the upper soft palate at the back of their mouth. Remember, it's breastfeeding NOT nipple feeding.

6. If they are making clicking noises and/or sucking their cheeks in, take baby off the boob (see above) and try again. Their cheeks should look full and round.

7. Make sure they are swallowing. This will often be frequent at the beginning of a feed and then slows down as they relax and move on from the thirst-quenching milk at the start to the thicker, fattier milk that follows.

8. If you choose to combination feed, try not to use a bottle before you have established your breastfeeding as it can cause baby some confusion because of the shape as well as the speed of the milk delivery.

9. If you feel you need a boost for your milk supply, check out our lactation cookies, opposite, our Breastfeeding Buddy smoothie (on page 67) and the teas on page 75.

10. Finally, if you are feeling stressed because the baby is struggling to latch on, hand baby over to partner, or put them in their crib and take five to calm down. When adrenaline is high, oxytocin levels cannot thrive and this will affect your ability to release milk for your baby. Try our simple calming breathing techniques (see pages 118–119) then try again when you feel more relaxed.

General breast care

We say if the latch is right then feeding shouldn't hurt, and while this is almost 100 per cent true, some people do have very sensitive nipples, and even with a great latch they can find the early breastfeeding days a little uncomfortable. Breast discomfort could also be due to inflammation from the friction of feeding, engorgement and blocked ducts. See our top ways to ease breast discomfort on pages 40–43. As with all things, if your symptoms are worsening or you feel unwell seek advice from your midwife, GP or a lactation consultant.

lactation cookies

Yes, we did say lactation cookies! Well, if you are going to eat a cookie, it might as well help with something, right? We must start by saying that the main factor for a good milk supply is attachment; if your latch is wrong, no number of cookies will help. However, if you have a good latch, but need a little boost for your supply, these cookies are believed to help!

Makes 16–20

230g butter, at room temperature
100g caster sugar
200g brown sugar
2 medium eggs
2 teaspoons vanilla extract
200g plain flour
½ teaspoon salt
½ teaspoon baking powder
3 tablespoons ground flaxseed
60g brewer's yeast
3 tablespoons almond, peanut or cashew nut butter (optional)
270g rolled oats
265g chocolate chips

Preheat the oven to 180°C/160°C fan. Line two baking sheets with parchment paper. Beat together the butter and sugars until light and fluffy. Beat in the eggs one at a time. Add the vanilla extract and beat to incorporate.

In a separate bowl, mix together the flour, salt, baking powder, ground flaxseed and brewer's yeast. Add to the wet ingredients and mix until combined. Stir in the almond butter (if using), oats and chocolate chips.

Roll 2 tablespoons of dough into a little ball and place on a lined baking sheet. Repeat with the rest of the dough.

Bake for 10–15 minutes, or until golden brown. Cool on the baking sheet for 10 minutes, then transfer to a wire rack to cool completely. Store in an air-tight container for up to a week or freeze for up to 3 months.

Responsive bottle feeding

If you are bottle feeding your little one with either expressed breast milk (EBM) or formula milk, you absolutely can still enjoy being close with them during feeds. You can still have skin-to-skin time as you bottle feed your baby and let that oxytocin flow, and this can have a lovely calming effect for the both of you.

If you are using formula milk, you may be trying to follow the instructions on the back of the packet exactly. But just remember that babies have no awareness of what these expectations are and will feed as and when they want.

As mentioned (see page 161), they only have little tummies (especially their first ten days) so if baby is not feeding exactly as the instructions suggest don't worry too much.
It may be that you aim to ultimately give your baby the same amount of feed over a 24-hour period as suggested on the pack, but you break the bottles up differently. For example, you may give them more frequent feeds, but a smaller amount for each.

Follow your baby, they will show you the way and you will learn all those lovely little feeding cues as the days and weeks pass. Let your baby tell you what they need and when they need it; after all, they are your BEST teacher. (See pages 149–150 for more on understanding your baby's cues.)

Top tips for getting through the night feeds

The night feeds can be hard, and it is something all mums are likely to find tricky sometimes. Let's face it, nobody really likes being woken up repeatedly from a lovely deep sleep. But babies need to feed frequently and this is just a part of early motherhood. Perhaps we'd embrace it better if we had a more realistic idea of the postnatal period, instead of being fed ideas about babies 'sleeping through' from a few weeks old. In many cultures, women learn that night feeding is an important and natural part of the postnatal period and are taught to enjoy this quiet, cosy feeding time with their babies!

We've listed some of our top tips below to help you embrace the nights, and hopefully even enjoy some night-time feeding.

1. **Keep the lights low.** This will stop you and baby waking up too much and will allow you to get back to sleep as quickly as possible.

2. **Make it as comfy as possible.** Try and feed baby in bed (if you have a bed nest or similar) or very near to the bed. If you have a feeding chair, make sure it is comfy and invest in a big snuggly blanket to wrap yourself in, so you don't get chilly. If it's very cold outside, consider some fluffy slippers or cosy slipper socks to keep your feet warm; cold feet can make getting back to sleep tricky!

3. **Take a flask of tea and a snack to bed.** In the early days, hormones mean we burn through calories quickly and tired tummies often feel hungry. Taking a warming flask of herbal or decaf tea to bed and having a low-sugar or sugar-free snack during the night feed can make you feel warm and cosy, helping you to get back to sleep quicker.

4. **Talking of flasks.** If you are bottle feeding, have a flask that is solely for feeds. At night, fill the flask with water at the right temperature for baby's feed and take it to the bedroom along with a couple of clean bottles and measured formula so that you have everything you need to quickly make up a feed in the night.

5. **Get even more organised.** Have everything you need close by to make the night time as easy as possible. Consider having a night-feed box by the bed, with wipes, nappies, breast pads . . . and this book!

6. **Be prepared for the night sweats.** The postnatal period brings with it an array of hormone changes to contend with, one of the most common side effects of which is 'night sweats'. If you are breastfeeding and adding leaky breasts into the mix, you may very well wake up with a clinging wet top. Having a dry top close by to quickly change into will help you get more comfortable so you can drift back to sleep.

7. **Pretend you're on hols, and embrace the siesta.** However you dress it up, broken sleep sucks. While we can make the night feeds as cosy as possible, being woken up in the night will take its toll if you don't look after yourself. The best way to do this is to sleep when you can in the day. A good old post-lunch siesta will mean you'll actually be able to stay awake long enough to eat your dinner in the evening!

WHAT IF I CAN'T BREASTFEED?

Sometimes, for many, many different reasons, breastfeeding just isn't working for mum or baby. This can be incredibly hard on a tired, vulnerable new mum and often comes with a truck load of guilt and feelings of failure. Perhaps you were desperate to breastfeed, but try as you might you just can't, or perhaps for your own reasons you felt that breastfeeding was not something you could or wanted to do, but felt pressured to by those around you to give it a go. Whatever your story is, we want you to stop beating yourself up. You should not feel guilty and you are absolutely not a failure — you are a wonderful new mum, who is doing the best she can for her beautiful new baby, and that is absolutely enough!

What we do know, is that lots of mamas who have been unable to breastfeed have worried about the affect this will have on their bonding with their baby. Let us reassure you that you will bond with your baby, when you feel happy, calm and supported, and if this isn't how you are feeling in your breastfeeding journey, the chances are that this is not helping you to bond at all! If bottle feeding your baby ends up being the choice that is right for you, then remember there are still lovely ways to encourage responsive bottle feeding (see page 166) which mimics breastfeeding. And we encourage new mums to have skin-to-skin while bottle feeding so that baby is still getting some lovely contact with you. Your job now is to stop feeling bad about this, stop comparing yourself to other mums and celebrate the wonderful job you are doing as a mother, caring for your baby and responding to their needs.

Let's Get Physical

In the first few weeks after birth, we advise women to rest, move regularly on their way to and from the bathroom and have a little stretch to get the blood flowing, but nothing more. We advise lifting nothing heavier than the baby, and to avoid high-impact, high-intensity exercise completely. In the early weeks, not only will exercise leave you tired and depleted, but because of the elevated levels of hormones making your muscles laxer, you can actually cause yourself some damage.

We are not saying don't move at all. On the contrary, gentle movement and gentle stretching will make you feel great, get the blood flowing, ease tired tense muscles, and encourage the release of endorphins and oxytocin. But movement should be gentle and restorative. You can do more vigorous exercise later, when relaxin levels are lower, bleeding has stopped (or become very light) your stitches are healed and you feel up to it. If you have had a Caesarean birth, you will need to be checked by your caregiver before resuming your exercise regime.

There are two things that you need to think about before embarking on an exercise programme: Is my core strong enough? And is my pelvic floor ready? Actually, the two go hand in hand. If your core muscles are struggling, you will be weaker in your pelvic floor. Until you are strong in the core, you will not be able to exercise safely. (See pages 19 and 26–27 for more on your pelvic floor.)

In theory, you are considered perfectly fine to get back to exercise from week 6, after your check up with the GP. However, in our experience, not many women have their abdomens checked at this appointment. It is important to ensure that if the recti muscles separated during pregnancy, that have contracted back postnatally, and to ensure your core is strong enough to support exercise. If you can, visit a women's health physio for a quick once over before starting exercising again to confirm that you are all set and ready to go. If you find you do have some separation in the abdominal muscles, we advise attending some postnatal Pilates classes. Many are specifically focused on restoring the core, and the teacher will be able to show you how to exercise carefully to help this separation come back together.

Many women joke about not being able to run or exercise without leaking a little bit of pee. While it is fairly common, it is your body's way of letting you know that all is not as strong as it should be in those core muscles. Stop your normal exercise regime, hit the Pilates core-restore work and once you are all zipped up, you can go back to your old exercise programme wee-free!

Sometimes classes don't allow you to take your baby, or perhaps it's hard to find a time that suits. Don't worry, there are some fab courses online that you can do while baby naps in the comfort of your own living room.

Exercise in the postnatal period can be a really confusing topic though. The most important thing is not to feel under any pressure. We think the following is a good estimate for the kinds of activity you might want to take part in at different stages of your recovery, but always go with what feels right for your body.

Week 1: Stay in bed!

Rest with your baby, and have plenty of skin-to-skin. Make sure you get up and walk around every couple of hours to get the blood flowing. This can be walking to the loo or to the kettle to make a cuppa. Then get back into bed!

Week 2: Move to the sofa!

Carry on resting up on the sofa with lots of skin-to-skin with your baby. Get up and walk to the loo, the kitchen for a snack and a cuppa, or just stretch your legs every couple of hours to keep the circulation moving.

Weeks 3–6: Gently does it

If you feel up to it and you have had a straightforward delivery with no stitches, then you can start going for some walks outside or doing some kitchen dancing to raise the heart rate a little and get the blood flowing. This will also encourage the release of oxytocin. Relaxin is high now and your joints, ligaments and pelvis are loose so don't overstretch or jerk your body around. You can also do our lovely gentle stretches on pages 46–52 – stick to the ones in this book for now as we know they are gentle enough for those loose ligaments and aren't going to strain sensitive parts.

Weeks 6–9: To the core

If you feel able, start doing some postnatal Pilates or postnatal yoga, and focusing on strengthening up the core muscles. If you suffered with any hypermobility or pelvic pain in the pregnancy, be very careful not to overstretch into your yoga poses; Pilates may be better for you while the relaxin is still quite high.

Week 9+

If your core muscles and pelvic floor are feeling strong, you can think about getting back into some more vigorous exercise. But if you're not there yet, don't push yourself! You're still so early in your postnatal journey. Carry on with Pilates to build your core strength.

yoga for the postnatal body

Yoga is a great reminder to move our bodies, stretch away aches and pains, remember to breathe, calm the mind and take time out to look after ourselves. So we asked pregnancy and postnatal yoga teacher Jane Grogan to put together a short, easy sequence that you can do at home in your PJs from week 6, to gently move and release your body and calm your mind. Enjoy!

If you have practised yoga before, you may find postnatal yoga completely different. This sequence is specifically designed to be gentle and releasing on the body. Yoga helps to teach us acceptance, to find calm in a storm despite any distractions, bringing us back to the breath. It encourages us to let go of the past and not look to the future but to just be present and focused on the here and now. Set out a comfortable area with a mat, some cushions, maybe play some relaxing tunes. Enjoy doing this yoga sequence alone or have someone read it aloud to you to guide you through the practice.

This sequence is made up of gentle restorative poses. Breathe deep, long and smooth breaths, in and out through your nose, throughout the practice. Pause between poses to allow time to reflect on how you are feeling.

Practise what you can, when you can. Try to let go of expectations of what you can achieve; maybe just try one or two poses to begin with. Savasana (rest pose) is always a great pose to make time for.

Supta Baddha Konasana
Reclining bound angle pose (supported)

Lie on your back with your knees bent and opened out like a butterfly, knees resting on cushions. Place one hand on your heart and the other on your belly. Focus on your heart and feel your breath. Allow your breath to become long, slow and steady. Breathe into the hand on your belly, feel it rise on the inhale and fall on the exhale.

Take several deep breaths here and notice how the body feels.

Mantra to repeat to yourself: I inhale calmness, I exhale stress and tension.

Pelvic tilts
Lie on your back with your knees bent, and place your feet flat on the floor underneath the knees and hip distance apart.

Place your arms down beside your body, palms facing up. Tuck your chin in slightly, creating a long neck pressing down gently into the floor.

Inhale and tilt your pelvis away from the front ribs, creating a small arch in the lower spine and pressing your tailbone into the floor.

Exhale and tilt your pelvis towards your rib cage. Lower spine moves towards the floor, tailbone curls under and hips are grounded. Repeat 5–10 times, creating a gentle rocking motion of the pelvis. This movement should be fluid and in time with the breath. Notice how you use your abdominal muscles in this exercise.

Mantra:
I am connected to the earth. I am connected to my body. I am not alone, we are one.

Chakravakasana
'Cat and cow'

Bring yourself on to all fours, hands in line with your shoulders, knees in line with your hips, keeping a neutral spine.

Move slowly, breathing deeply and matching your movement to your breath.

Inhale, allow the chest to expand. Belly drops downwards with light abdominal engagement, head lifts in line with spine and tailbone tilts towards the sky.

Exhale, begin to draw the belly in towards the spine, movement flows through neutral and into a curve.

Connect through the hands pressing gently into the floor as your back domes. Press between the shoulder blades, head drops naturally, pelvis gently tucks under. Follow the exhale fully, abs engage, squeezing the breath from the body.

Repeat 5–7 times.

Mantra:
Inhale, I am opening my heart and the energy which surrounds it. My feelings may be expressed and released. Exhale, I am protected, my awareness moves inward for introspection.

Supported Balasana
'Child's pose'

Come to a kneeling position with feet flat, toes together and your bottom resting on your heels, with hips relaxed. Place a bolster or cushions between the knees that reaches far enough forwards so when you fold the upper body from the hips, you can turn the head and place one ear down on to the cushions/bolster. Rest the arms, reaching slightly forwards either side, elbows down.

Lengthen and extend the arms on the inhale, soften and relax the arms on the even exhale.

Mantra:
I am present. I listen to the sound of my breath, I feel the beat of my heart. I listen.

Savasana
'Rest pose'

On your back, bring your arms beside your body. Draw the shoulder blades inwards and allow the chest to widen. Lengthen the pelvis downwards away from body, and allow the lower spine to settle into the floor. Legs as wide as the mat, toes drop outwards. Wrap yourself in a blanket if you wish. Close the eyes and find stillness in your body. Deeply relax and stay here for a few minutes, or as long as you need to.

Staying in touch with the calm and focus from savasana, come out of the pose slowly. Roll to one side before you're ready to bring yourself up.

Mantra:
I am grounded. I am relaxed. I am whole.

Back in the Sack

So, you've been sent home from hospital, or been discharged from the midwife, with a bag full of condoms and a reminder that you can actually get pregnant when breastfeeding, so it would be wise to use a barrier method until you work out what other form of contraception you'd like to use! Your chin falls to the floor and you think 'I am NEVER having sex again'! Fear not – you will! We've all been there . . . 'Have you done it yet?' seems to be a question asked a lot between friends and NCT groups, and as a midwife and doula we are constantly asked questions such as 'When is it okay to have sex?' 'When will I feel like having sex?' and, most commonly, 'WILL I ever feel like having sex again?'

FIRST THINGS FIRST: you've just birthed a baby. Whichever way your baby arrived and however long or short your birth was, the chances are, right now, you don't fancy anything else poking around down there, and that is perfectly fine! If you birthed vaginally, you'll be feeling a little sore and swollen down below. If you birthed your baby via Caesarean section, you'll probably be very sore and bloated in your tummy (with terrible wind . . . It's not your fault, it happens to every C-section mum, it's because you've been pumped full of air; 'Better out than in,' we say). You're likely to be sore down below too due to shifting post-pregnancy hormones. (See our section on Easing Sore Parts on pages 34–35 for how to soothe this delicate area.)

Saying that, we have had clients who have felt quite up for 'it' straight after birth, experiencing an oxytocin high and feeling more connected than ever with their partner through sharing such a wonderful experience together. If you feel like this, congratulations! But it is still advised that you wait around two to four weeks before intercourse, until bleeding has stopped, otherwise you can be at a higher risk of haemorrhage and infection. If you have had a tear or episiotomy and stitches then it is advised that you wait until your six- week check with the GP.

Although you may have been given the medical go-ahead, we actually think six weeks is an unrealistic timeframe, and in our experience, most of our ladies are not ready to resume a physical relationship with their partners until around twelve to sixteen weeks. There is no rush, and no right or wrong time, only what feels right for you and your partner. Just let that reconnection happen at a pace you feel comfortable with and keep talking about it together.

Okay, so your bits are all healed, and your tummy less sore and bloated, so why are you still not feeling up for a bit of hanky panky? HORMONES!! These little blighters have a big part to play in whether or not we are feeling up for some sexy time! Just after birth, we have a dip in our sexy hormones and a rise in prolactin (the hormone for milk production) which is known to supress libido. This is probably nature's way of giving us some time to heal. In many cultures around the world, women have bed rest for weeks after childbirth and sex is not allowed, as mother's focus is on healing and feeding her baby.

As well as this, adjusting to becoming a mother – or adapting to your growing family – can be extremely overwhelming. Combined with tiredness and anxiety this can also result in our bodies producing large quantities of adrenaline. Adrenaline tells us we are in danger – not particularly conducive to having sex! The hormone that makes us feel sexy is in fact the same hormone that helps birth flow well: good old oxytocin, the hormone of love. It makes us feel all warm and fuzzy, and in the right conditions, with enough time and space to relax, up for a bit of the other.

So how do we get more oxytocin and less adrenaline? Good question. Below are some ways to encourage oxytocin production, reconnect physically with your partner and feel more in the mood. At the very least you will feel more relaxed and less stressed! (Also see pages 113–116 and 129–130 for how to deal with those feelings of anxiety and overwhelm.)

- **Spend some time together.** Just spending time with your partner can help you feel less frazzled and more connected to each other. This doesn't have to be out of the house and away from the baby, even a cheeky glass of bubbles in the bath together while baby is napping can be a wonderful little get away! Leave the dishes, ignore the mess and get that bath running!

- **Get naked!** Skin-to-skin is not just for mum and baby, it's great for couples too. Lying naked together, having skin to skin will raise your oxytocin levels and help you feel more relaxed and sexual. Even if you don't actually have sex, you will both benefit from the emotional connection and chemical hormonal reaction of skin-to-skin. If you are just too plain tired, sleep naked, and enjoy the feeling of your partner's skin against yours as you rest.

- **Exercise.** We know when you are tired this is the last thing you feel like doing, but paradoxically, the more you exercise, the more energy you will have. The wonderful side effect of exercise is that we produce endorphins, which make us feel happy. When we feel happy we are much more likely to be up for some fun. Take a walk, have a dance, do some gentle stretches or anything that will get your heart rate up and your blood pumping (see pages 171–173 for advice on exercising, pages 46–52 for our simple stretches, and pages 174–177 for a restorative yoga sequence).

- **Laugh.** Laughter, as they say, is the best medicine! Laughing is good for the soul on so many levels, it makes us feel happy, free and of course fills us up with the lovely hormone oxytocin. Try and have a giggle with your partner, watch a funny video together, or a favourite comedian and enjoy the lovely feeling you get from having a laugh. See page 185 on how to keep your humour!

- **Masturbation.** This can be a great way to ease yourself gently back into the world of sex. Take your time and remind yourself how to enjoy your body in that way.

- **Change of scenery.** Take yourself out for an hour or two, on your own, or with your partner and little one. If you don't feel like going out, sleep in a different room, or camp out in the lounge. A change of scenery can be very stimulating and energising for the brain.

Learning to love and embrace your postnatal body will also help you to feel more confident about jumping back in the sack (see pages 89–93 for more on body image). If you are breastfeeding and leaky breasts are throwing you off your game, consider wearing a bra or crop top during the fun to boundary off the area.

Becoming a parent is a busy time and it does help to get organised and schedule stuff in, even sex! Crazy as that may seem, if it's in the diary, you can plan for it, get ready for it and even look forward to it, and of course, if the time comes and you are too tired, or the baby won't sleep, like all diary dates, you can reschedule. Try out Fornication Friday, Sexy Saturday or Sensual Sunday! A lot of mums worry that baby will wake up during the deed, if this happens, try and keep a sense of humour about it, you can always book in a 'to be continued' session soon.

Relax . . .

Anxious muscles contract and tighten. Tight muscles don't allow for easy penetration and can make intercourse feel painful, which makes you tense up even more! Don't worry, luckily there are some easy ways to lessen the tension, relax the muscles and make things easier.

- **Have a bath.** Soak in a warm bath – the warm water will relax the muscles and the time out will help you to switch off and relax.

- **Relax your jaw.** Either give yourself a little jaw massage in the bath – or prepare yourself a drink with a straw in, and sip away! You can't suck on a straw with a tight jaw, so with each sip the jaw has to relax. You could even make it a cheeky G&T if that tickles your fancy.

- **Skin-to-skin.** This will create oxytocin which will in turn relax muscles (see page 180).

- **Open your mouth.** We know it sounds crazy right, but if you open your mouth as your partner penetrates, it will help you to open up in the vagina too. Breathe out with an 'ohhhhhh' or an 'ahhhhhh' and you will physically relax your muscles down below at the same time.

- **Have a massage.** Ask your partner to give you a massage, this will help your muscles to relax and soften and will help you to mentally switch off your brain from the day (see pages 56–58).

- **Lube!** Another cause of discomfort during intercourse can be vaginal dryness due to the lower postnatal levels of oestrogen. Nothing that some good old-fashioned lube won't help with. However, don't use the good old-fashioned stuff, because it's full of harsh chemicals that can leave you with more discomfort than you started out with. Instead opt for an organic lube, you'll find lots online. Ensure that you are using a water-based lubricant as anything oil-based can weaken the latex of a condom, and cause it to break!

What if this isn't your first baby?

If this isn't your first baby, you will have no doubt been dealing with all the emotions that come with having a second (third, fourth?) baby. Will I have enough love to go around? Will my eldest be okay? Will I be able to cope? The answer is: yes!

Often, we are so focused on all the things that might be tricky, that we forget the joy that a new baby can bring to the family. Older siblings will often relish their new role as big brother or sister, and will enjoy being allied with their parents in the role of caring for the new baby.

If you find you are feeling a bit torn in all directions trying to be all things to all people, try and make sure you have some one-to-one time put aside for each child during the week. Try having a regular café or park date with your elder children without the baby, and let this be a time where they have your undivided attention. We often find that as mums, we need this time even more than they do!

- Play a fun and silly board game.
- Draw/paint/scrapbook.
- Take a walk to the local shop with a little shopping bag so they feel like your special little helper.
- Play hide and seek together.
- Take a bath together and have fun having a bit of a splash about.
- Snuggle up underneath a cosy blanket on the sofa and read them a few of their favourite stories, including the silliest voices you can muster and watch their faces light up.

TOP 5 WAYS TO KEEP A SENSE OF HUMOUR

Becoming a parent, as wonderful as it may be, can be really hard! Amidst the wakeful nights, parenting learning curves and finding your new mama identity, it's really important to try and keep a sense of humour. Here are our top five ways to keep on laughing through it all.

1. LAUGH ALONG WITH OTHERS GOING THROUGH IT TOO

There are lots of bloggers and vloggers out there sharing their parenting highs and lows with brilliant humour. Sometimes, on the bad days it can help to hear other people sharing their tricky times with comedic delivery to make us realise that, actually, sometimes, just sometimes, it's better to laugh than cry over this stuff!

2. PHONE A FRIEND

Most of us have a friend we can count on to pull us out of the doldrums and make us see the funny side of life. When you feel like you can't raise a smile, call them up and tell them you need cheering up. Sometimes, just recounting the hardships of the day to somebody on the outside is enough to make us see it all a little differently and have enough distance to see the funny side.

3. WATCH SOMETHING FUNNY

A funny clip, video, vlog, or a movie you know makes you laugh and feel better — whack it on and distract yourself with some comedy for five minutes and allow yourself to have a giggle.

4. REMEMBER TOMORROW IS ANOTHER DAY

We need to remember that tomorrow is another day, with the hope of a better day! Sometimes, this can relieve the pressure we are feeling enough for us to view a situation objectively and see the funny side.

5. REMEMBER YOU ARE NOT ALONE

Somewhere across the globe, and quite possibly in a house not too far away from you right now, is another mum dealing with a cranky baby, a projectile puke or leaking boobs just like you! Feel the cosmic sisterhood, laugh in the face of poonamis and remember: you, and women all over the world right now, have got this!

a final word

Throughout the years, we have had the absolute honor of working closely with many postnatal women as they adapt and navigate their way through the incredible early days (and months) of motherhood. We are so grateful that through this book we have also been able to play a small part in your mothering story, as you heal and adjust, both physically and mentally, to life on the other side of birthing a baby.

As women we give so much of our body, mind and energy to our little ones throughout pregnancy, birth and the postnatal period. During this busy life change, we sometimes forget just how much we matter too, and that integrating and carving out time to practise self-care in our lives every day is not self-indulgent, but absolutely essential. In so many cultures all over the world, women are celebrated and nurtured after they have birthed their babies, and we want you to feel supported too.

We hope that the information, tips and guidance here on these pages have helped you understand what is happening to your incredible body, as it once again shifts gear and works hard to return to a pre-pregnant state.

There are so many practical and nurturing ways you can support yourself as you journey through this period of motherhood and we have aimed to share these with you in a way that is easy to access, in bite-sized chunks so that you can get hold of the advice and information that you need, promptly and easily, as and when you need it.

As you continue through this extraordinary time as a new mum, pop this little book somewhere you can find it easily and have a quick flick through whenever you need advice, information and practical ways to help your body heal, calm your mind or just provide a torch to follow on the days you need a little extra guiding.

Whether you are looking for practical ways to support your mind and body, quick pick-me-ups when you are having 'one of those days' (we all have them) or little fist bumps for the days you are feeling a bit flat, it's all here in this book to remind you that, bit by bit, you are getting there, trusting yourself more and finding your feet on your very own motherhood journey. In short, you are nailing it!

As mothers ourselves who work with mothers, we know first-hand what a rollercoaster the postnatal period can be. Some days we are full to bursting with love and pride and we want to celebrate it all and other days we are treading water and need holding a little bit tighter.

We never want you to feel that you are alone on this great adventure. Right now so many women are out there going through a very similar experience to you. The highs, the challenges, the elation and the tears are all important parts of the emotional patchwork of this incredible period in our lives.

We always say: you can't pour from an empty cup, and we mean it. Be kind and gentle with yourself and remember that you matter, and that by taking care of yourself, you're filling up that tank, so that you can give even more to your little one.

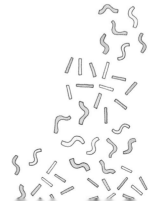

Index:

Resources

Breastfeeding
www.abm.me.uk
www.breastfeedingnetwork.org.uk
www.imogenunger.com
www.laleche.org.uk
www.lcgb.org
www.nationalbreastfeedinghelpline.org.uk
www.tongue-tie.org.uk

Responsive bottle feeding
www.firststepsnutrition.org
www.guiltfreebottlefeeding.com
www.fearlessformulafeeder.com

Mental health – Postnatal depression and anxiety support
www.apni.org (The Association for Postnatal Illness)
www.mind.org.uk
www.nhs.uk/conditions/stress-anxiety-depression/mental-health-helplines
www.pandasfoundation.org.uk
www.postpartumprogress.com
www.samaritans.org – 08457 909090 (24 hours)

Birth debriefing
www.birthtraumaassociation.org.uk
www.doctoranddaughter.co.uk

Wellbeing
Calm meditations: www.mindfulmotherhood.org
Herbalist, Jo Farren: www.farrensherbal.co.uk
Mindfulness: www.headspace.com
Positive affirmations: www.londonhypnobirthing.co.uk
Postnatal exercise, Emma Fullwood: www.superchargedclub.co.uk
Postnatal exercise/diastasis help: www.mutusystem.com
Postnatal physiotherapy: www.uclh.nhs.uk

General help and support
www.doula.org.uk
www.nightnannies.com

Finding other local mums
www.letsmush.com
www.meetup.com
www.mumstheword.online
www.peanut-app.io

Thank you! ♥

First and foremost, thank you to our brilliant publisher, Sam Jackson, who put her faith in us because she understands how tough those early days can be and had the insight to realise that this book was needed.

Thank you to our very talented editor, Laura Herring, who just knows how to take what is written and make it clear, user-friendly and articulate – and always spots the mistakes we miss with her magical eagle eye.

A big thank you to our wonderfully creative designer, Laura Liggins, who has turned a monochrome manuscript into the stylish little hardback you see today.

Thank you to our dear friend and illustrator, Kay Barker, who worked tirelessly to fill this book with such beautiful, thoughtful and sensitive illustrations. Kay, you make us look much cooler then we really are and we love you heaps.

A huge thank you to Hollie McNish for allowing us to have what we think is THE best poem for a new mum ever in our book – Megatron, from her brilliant book Nobody Told Me.

Thank you to Jane Grogan, Jo Farren and Emma Fullwood for contributing to this book with their expertise and thank you to all of the mums who shared their stories with us that are scattered in the book.

Alexis would also like to thank: Jean, Amy, Denise and Gemma who taught me SO much about being the best midwife possible. Thanks, mum, for every single little way you have nurtured and supported me throughout my life. Big love to my three children, who enriched my life and who have been so patient letting mummy write this little book. And huge love and thanks to my husband, Dan, who has been my safe base and biggest cheerleader since we met back at school. Thank you for looking after our three littles so I could crack on and write this book.

Beccy says thank you to: Michelle Odent, Lilliana Llamers and Suzanne Yates – learning with you all was a total inspiration. Thank you to all my friends and family for your constant support and belief in me. Special thanks to my husband, Barney, and my amazing daughters, Ella and Isabel, for all your love, support and brilliant humour, for putting up with me being 'on call' and dashing off to births, and being patient with me while writing this book.

Finally, we'd like to say a huge thank you to all of the women who have allowed us to support them on their amazing motherhood journey over the years. We learn so much from you all and it is an absolute honour, always. If it wasn't for all of you, we wouldn't be here doing what we are doing today!